On
Talent

HBR's 10 Must Reads series is the definitive collection of ideas and best practices for aspiring and experienced leaders alike. These books offer essential reading selected from the pages of *Harvard Business Review* on topics critical to the success of every manager.

Titles include:

HBR's 10 Must Reads 2015
HBR's 10 Must Reads 2016
HBR's 10 Must Reads 2017
HBR's 10 Must Reads 2018
HBR's 10 Must Reads 2019
HBR's 10 Must Reads 2020
HBR's 10 Must Reads 2021
HBR's 10 Must Reads 2022
HBR's 10 Must Reads for CEOs
HBR's 10 Must Reads for New Managers
HBR's 10 Must Reads on AI, Analytics, and the New Machine Age
HBR's 10 Must Reads on Boards
HBR's 10 Must Reads on Building a Great Culture
HBR's 10 Must Reads on Business Model Innovation
HBR's 10 Must Reads on Career Resilience
HBR's 10 Must Reads on Change Management (Volumes 1 and 2)
HBR's 10 Must Reads on Collaboration
HBR's 10 Must Reads on Communication (Volumes 1 and 2)
HBR's 10 Must Reads on Creativity
HBR's 10 Must Reads on Design Thinking
HBR's 10 Must Reads on Diversity
HBR's 10 Must Reads on Emotional Intelligence
HBR's 10 Must Reads on Entrepreneurship and Startups
HBR's 10 Must Reads on High Performance
HBR's 10 Must Reads on Innovation
HBR's 10 Must Reads on Leadership (Volumes 1 and 2)
HBR's 10 Must Reads on Leadership for Healthcare

On
Talent

HARVARD BUSINESS REVIEW PRESS
Boston, Massachusetts

The web addresses referenced in this book were live and correct at the time of the book's publication but may be subject to change.

Library of Congress Cataloging-in-Publication Data

Names: Harvard Business Review Press, issuing body.
Title: HBR's 10 must reads on talent / Harvard Business Review.
Other titles: Harvard business review's ten must reads on talent | HBR's 10 must reads (Series)
Description: Boston, Massachusetts : Harvard Business Review Press, [2022] | Series: HBR's 10 must reads | Includes index. |
Identifiers: LCCN 2022021851 (print) | LCCN 2022021852 (ebook) | ISBN 9781647824587 (paperback) | ISBN 9781647824594 (epub)
Subjects: LCSH: Personnel management. | Success in business. | Ability.
Classification: LCC HF5549 .H3679 2022 (print) | LCC HF5549 (ebook) | DDC 658.3—dc23/eng/20220804
LC record available at https://lccn.loc.gov/2022021851
LC ebook record available at https://lccn.loc.gov/2022021852

ISBN: 978-1-64782-458-7
eISBN: 978-1-64782-459-4

The paper used in this publication meets the requirements of the American National Standard for Permanence of Paper for Publications and Documents in Libraries and Archives Z39.48-1992.

Contents

On
Talent

Building a Game-Changing Talent Strategy

by Douglas A. Ready, Linda A. Hill, and Robert J. Thomas

FOUNDED 25 YEARS AGO by eight partners, BlackRock, the world's largest asset management firm, rewrote the playbook in financial services. While many of its peers were stumbling and retrenching in the aftermath of the 2008 recession, BlackRock was charting a course for growth. Its revenue, profits, and stock price all performed consistently during that tumultuous period.

What interests us is that the company continues to excel. It has a palpable sense of pride—a buzz. But what makes it different? BlackRock is driven by an explicit and concrete mission: "To create a better financial future for our clients." It excels at commercializing innovation. Its technology platform, Aladdin (Asset Liability and Debt & Derivative Investment Network), boasts the world's most sophisticated risk-analytics capabilities combined with superior functionality in portfolio administration, trading, and data control and operations. BlackRock is maniacally focused on delivering high performance, and its leaders say they are proud that the firm's 11,000-plus professionals abide by its four guiding principles: to be fiduciaries to its clients, to be passionate about performance, to be innovators, and to be "one BlackRock."

We looked at BlackRock and two other companies that have reshaped their respective industries—one Indian and one Chinese (see sidebars)—and found significant commonalities. Although these companies vary widely in scope, scale, and maturity, they demonstrate the essential attributes of a game-changing organization: They are *purpose-driven, performance-oriented,* and *principles-led.* And in the process of conducting interviews at these companies, we discovered a thread that weaves them even more tightly together: All three have superior talent strategies.

The Mechanics Behind the Magic

From our decades of experience as both researchers and advisers, it's clear what sets those talent strategies apart: They are relentlessly focused on supporting, and in some cases driving, the companies' business strategies. They are comprehensive, addressing group, divisional, regional, and business unit considerations. They add value, and they work exceptionally well.

Commitment from the top executive team is central to building and maintaining this business-first mindset. Game-changing leaders not only excel at articulating the vital importance of talent management but also are heavily engaged in their companies' actual practices. They demand that their line leaders be accountable for spotting, developing, and retaining the next generation of leaders.

That commitment is essential to recruitment—the next important building block in a superior talent strategy. Seasoned HR professionals have little patience for executives who talk a good game about the importance of human assets but then cut management and professional development at the first sign of thinning margins. Line leaders who are skeptical about making substantial and continual investments in their people have already lost the war for talent. A division president recently said to one of us during a strategic offsite, "We don't need to waste time building a strong HR team, and certainly not a fancy talent strategy—that's what headhunters are for!" His company is currently fighting for its life, largely because it didn't invest in finding and developing the right people to execute its vision and strategy.

Idea in Brief

The Insight

Game-changing organizations are purpose-driven, performance-oriented, and principles-led—and they have talent strategies that guide and even drive their business strategies.

The Analysis

Those talent strategies balance four inherent tensions: They support both strategic and operational superiority; they are globally scaled yet locally relevant; they foster a collective culture yet enable high potentials to thrive as individuals; and their policies endure yet are agile and open to revitalization.

The Payoff

Mastering all four tensions will help your organization stay focused on its core purpose, build a high-performance culture, and follow guiding principles that are authentic and energizing.

Committed line leaders and gifted HR managers together create an organizational climate of spirit and energy—a magnet for the very best professionals. Their talent policies are built to last but are constantly under review, to ensure that they can respond to changing conditions on the ground and to cultural differences across the globe.

Getting these things right makes all the difference. It creates an authentic connection between how a company presents itself as an employer and how it really feels inside—the employee value proposition. It gives a healthy sense that promises made are promises kept. Authenticity paves the way for transparency. When employees know what it takes to perform, develop, grow, and succeed, they trust that their company is a meritocracy.

Make no mistake: This is not an easy place to get to. In fact, the path to a truly game-changing talent strategy is rife with complexity and ambiguity. How can both strategy and execution be consistently superior? How can they support a collective culture yet enable high potentials to thrive as individuals? How can the strategy be global and local at the same time? And how can its policies endure yet be agile and constantly open to revitalization? Too many organizations end up making zero-sum decisions when faced with

Envision Energy

Purpose and Professional Development

When Lei Zhang founded Envision, in 2007, his goal was to revolutionize the energy industry—to create a company that would "help solve the challenges of a sustainable future for mankind." Unlike most other Chinese companies, Envision would compete on technology rather than on cost of labor.

To achieve his goals, Lei knew, he had to approach talent sourcing and development differently. The design and manufacture of wind turbines is highly interdisciplinary and technologically sophisticated, and his software platform required deep know-how in both energy management and information technology. Lei set out to source his employees globally and across industries and to attract individuals with world-class capabilities.

Lei and Jerry Luo, Envision's vice president for HR, were convinced that many successful executives were searching for a greater sense of meaning in their work—a big and exciting idea to lead the industry forward—and that's what they offered. They wanted employees who could work across cultures and who had an "open innovation" mindset, so they confined their recruiting to people with multinational experience. They took their search to global pockets of excellence: to Denmark for engineers with alternative-energy-innovation skills, to the United States for software architects, and to Japan for managers skilled in lean manufacturing techniques. They attracted an exceptionally diverse range of top performers.

Talent development was central to Envision's strategy. Lei and Luo devised an approach based on three integrated pillars: the Talent and Development Challenge System, which enables employees to solve increasingly difficult technical challenges, acquire additional responsibility, and create internal and external value; 36 behavioral indicators of developmental "accelerators"— namely, "wisdom, will, and love"; and a 360-degree feedback system.

Lei and Luo were determined to create opportunity for everyone. "Envision is here to help people achieve their ambitions and to help improve the world," Luo says. So far, their efforts are paying off: Envision's revenue has doubled every year since its founding.

such challenges. One trap a company might fall into is to think that because it's a global company, its talent practices need to be globally consistent as a matter of fairness.

Game-changers don't look at these issues as trade-offs. Rather, they see them as inherent tensions that must be carefully managed and reconciled: A strategic orientation must be balanced by ruthless operational efficiency; a sense of collectiveness must be balanced by the need for individuals to build their careers; a global perspective must be balanced by local relevance; enduring commitments must leave room for regeneration and renewal. Mastering all four of these tensions together will help your organization achieve and maintain high performance.

Strategic and Operational

Superior strategic insight is critical for creating that all-important distance between a company and its competition. Yet the current environment is so intense that winning can come down to a company's ability to execute more effectively than its rivals. Finding a balance between constant strategic agility and dependable operational excellence is tough for many organizations.

The same holds true for game-changing talent strategies. An innovative business model requires that the very best talent be sourced, engaged, developed, and retained. Having a great model is hard enough; finding outstanding talent to execute it is even more challenging, particularly in emerging markets.

Putting the right talent in the right roles at the right time is one of the differentiators that keep BlackRock out in front. Its talent management policies and practices are guided by its global Human Capital Committee, composed of 35 senior line leaders from across the firm's businesses and key locations. The only HCC member from HR is Jeff Smith, the global head of human resources; he cochairs the committee with Ken Wilson, a BlackRock vice chairman and a highly respected leader in the financial services industry. Both are members of the firm's Global Executive Committee. The HCC's very existence sends a powerful message that talent is not only a strategic and scarce resource but a matter of critical accountability for line management.

Charged with protecting the firm's one-company culture, the HCC ensures that the four guiding principles shape day-to-day operations and behaviors and helps guide every aspect of what might be viewed

5

as a talent management value chain across the company. Here are its responsibilities:

Talent planning and recruitment

Although the HCC leaves talent tracking and workforce planning to the leaders of the various businesses, it is actively engaged in employer branding. Recognizing that the firm needed to tailor its appeal to a new breed of college and business school graduates, members of the HCC worked with the marketing team to devise a campus recruiting campaign that addresses two of the highest priorities among young people: career mobility and social responsibility.

Ensuring a high-performance culture

Line leaders at BlackRock own the employee engagement process, but the HCC leads focus groups to identify ways of enhancing employees' experience throughout the firm. It has also raised performance standards and improved the firm's approach to identifying and promoting high-potential talent—by, for example, assessing leaders on their efforts in this regard.

Prioritizing leadership behaviors that matter

The HCC insisted that a core part of its charter be to protect and promote the culture and values of the firm by ensuring that leaders are assessed not only on their technical performance but also on how well they live by and teach the guiding principles. As Donnell Green, BlackRock's global head of talent management, puts it, "The HCC and BlackRock's Global Executive Committee are not afraid to address head-on some of the stickier issues of culture change and culture formation, including breaking down silo behavior and driving harder to create a stronger high-performance culture. We live our principles day in and day out. One of them is 'We are one BlackRock,' so leaders who try to make their numbers in a zero-sum fashion by undermining their colleagues soon find out that there is no place for them at the firm."

Tata Group

Talent Capture in Acquired Companies

Tata is India's largest enterprise group, with businesses in seven sectors, operations in some 80 countries, more than 450,000 employees, and revenue in excess of $100 billion. In recent years it has grown through a series of strategic acquisitions and joint ventures. Global growth and diversity have brought a complex mix of talent management challenges.

Tata's HR and talent organization has become skilled at determining the value (real and potential) of the people in the companies it acquires and at risk management and talent capture. Risk management involves assessing the culture of the acquired company. HR works alongside finance and strategy to ascertain "where the target company has come from" and how it has dealt with challenges in the past, says Satish Pradhan, who recently retired as executive vice president of group human resources. "You need to understand their fears, their drama, their anxieties." By providing insight into the acquired company's readiness for change and the distance between its culture and Tata's, the talent team helps mitigate risk. This process, which stretches through postmerger integration, can take 12 to 24 months.

Talent capture is all about unlocking the ambitions and the potential of a leadership team that may be dispirited by a history of challenging performance or subordination to short-term goals. Pradhan grew accustomed to stories of resignation and even despair: "They'd say things like 'Why don't you guys just tell us what you want us to do.'" When Tata sees opportunity in an acquisition candidate, it seeks to unlock potential at the outset by creating a shared vision: What does the company aspire to be, and how can Tata enable that aspiration? "Initially there is cynicism and disbelief and 'What are they not telling us? What's the game here?'" Pradhan says. "Then, over time, they realize that we are actually serious about what we're saying. We actually want the acquired company to have aspirations."

Developing employees

The HCC presides over a robust process of employee and managerial development. BlackRock leaders have long valued stretch assignments and bosses who pay attention to developing direct reports as cornerstones of the firm's talent philosophy. Feeling that one downside of being "a family" can be the impression that the firm's performance standards are lax, they realize the importance of targeted development. Managing at BlackRock is a program that helps executives be more effective coaches, delegators, and drivers of high performance. As managers move up through the ranks, they can take advantage of an array of programs, such as Driving Performance Through Teams, Influencing for Results, and Enterprise Leadership.

Talent reviews and succession planning

BlackRock has developed an extensive process for talent reviews and promotions. "The foundation of our business model is collaboration for the client," Green says, "so who gets promoted to leading at BlackRock matters a great deal." Green worked with the HCC to construct a talent review process that explicitly assesses employees on being collaborative leaders.

Networking and collaboration tools

The HCC uses The Block, BlackRock's online chat room and collaboration hub, and other types of communication to foster dialogue on subjects such as boosting innovation, networking with the firm's leaders from emerging markets, and strengthening engagement in growth priorities.

Collective and Individual

Our recent research makes clear the importance of creating companies that are guided by a collective sense of purpose. People have always sought meaning in their lives, but we found that a sense of purpose is an overwhelming differentiator in attracting top talent. At the same time, these professionals want opportunities to grow, exciting assignments, and interesting careers. A game-changing talent strategy helps companies provide all these elements.

Game-changers are clear about the purpose for which they exist. They know that performance is the route to remaining competitive. And they are adamant that their principles will see them through good times and bad. A company's talent managers can support its objectives by articulating up front that it demands enthusiastic buy-in to its core purpose. Nonbelievers need not apply.

Every game-changing company we know is backed by a powerful sense of collective pride and a respect for individuals' need to grow. "We are maniacal about driving high performance, but we are also a family," says Larry Fink, a cofounder of BlackRock and its CEO and chairman.

Collectivism, collaboration, trust, and respect are the foundation of BlackRock's belief system. "What makes a game-changer in my mind is that our clarity of purpose is crystal clear, has never changed, and never will," Fink says. "We are a fiduciary to our clients. We serve them. We never, ever compete with them." The notion of collective behavior was so important to BlackRock's founders that in its first few years they decided they'd all be paid the same. Thus everyone could focus on sharing information and working together to serve clients.

BlackRock also has a powerful tool for collaboration in Aladdin. "You need integrated pipes to keep a business together," Fink explains. "Aladdin does that for us. One platform means we are all looking at the same information together, in a transparent fashion, with every business we run and in every location throughout the world. This allows us to talk as 'we' and not 'they.' To be a successful leader at BlackRock, you need to be an exceptional sharer of information." Charlie Hallac, BlackRock's chief operating officer, adds, "I believe it's not possible to effectively represent the firm to our clients if we can't all articulate Aladdin's value to BlackRock."

BlackRock's leaders work to build the collective spirit. "We lead by example and then reinforce those examples through telling stories," says Rob Kapito, BlackRock's president and a cofounder. "Much of what makes BlackRock a special place is that we take our time to select the right partners and the right employees. The notion of 'we' dominates here. I bring our emerging leaders to my house. I cook for them. They get to know me as a person, not just a role. Trust is built by people being transparent and authentic with one another. Authenticity has high currency at BlackRock."

Global and Local

Nowadays it seems almost trite for a company to announce, "We are a global company, competing in a complex global environment."

Do You Have a Game-Changing Talent Strategy?

Thinking about the first three statements below should give your team an indication of what it needs to do to make your company a game-changer. The remaining statements should allow it to gauge to what extent your company's talent policies and practices are working in support of that objective.

1. My company places "purpose" at the heart of its business model.

2. My company has a high-performance culture.

3. Leaders in my company follow well-understood guiding principles.

4. Our people policies help drive our business strategy.

5. Our talent management practices are highly effective.

6. Our leaders are completely committed to excellence in talent management.

7. Our leaders are deeply engaged in and accountable for spotting, tracking, coaching, and developing the next generation of leaders.

8. Our talent practices are strategically oriented, but they also put a premium on operational efficiency.

9. Our talent practices engender a strong sense of collective purpose and pride yet work very well for my career as an individual.

10. Our talent practices strike the right balance between global scale and local responsiveness.

11. My company has a long-standing commitment to people development, but we are very open to changing our policies when circumstances dictate.

In reality, companies function as confederations of local entities—some of them operating with reasonable autonomy, and some deeply dependent on other businesses and regions—and in strategic partnerships with outside companies. Therefore, identifying, developing, engaging, and retaining local talent is of paramount importance to a company's success. Winning today has little to do with the efficacy of moving ex-pats in and out of local environments. Top performers who might once have aspired to the head office are now angling for leadership roles in their home countries.

But sometimes individuals want to move from their countries and regions, and sometimes a company simply needs to move its key resources. In those situations, game-changing companies know where their best people are, what capabilities they possess, and how they can help with the challenges the company is facing.

BlackRock's talent policies and practices are globally scaled and locally relevant. Its global graduate recruitment program is built on strong relationships with local universities and business schools. It has rolled out We Are One BlackRock and guiding-principles workshops in its offices around the world and made sure they were facilitated by local BlackRock leaders.

The firm's global brand and local relationships draw top senior talent to the firm. One example is Mark McCombe, formerly the CEO of HSBC Hong Kong, who joined BlackRock as its chairman, Asia Pacific. Another is Hsueh-ming Wang, a former Goldman Sachs partner, who recently joined as the first chair of BlackRock's China operations.

Enduring and Regenerative

In the top-performing companies, a sense of legacy and continuity matters. But talented individuals are drawn to organizations that continually refresh their systems and processes as well as their strategic initiatives, in order to delight customers and outwit competitors. Great companies know that by being agile they can stay in play for many years.

Perhaps the most powerful way to do this is by building a talent strategy that both endures and regenerates. Jeff Smith, BlackRock's global head of HR, came to the firm through its 2009 acquisition of Barclays Global Investors, when Fink and the Global Executive Committee decided that BGI's HR practices were better able to support their firm's priorities. BlackRock has gained strength and momentum—and many leaders—from each of its acquisitions; the GEC includes four from the BGI merger.

Smith and his team constantly scan for innovations in HR and talent management practices while ensuring that BlackRock's guiding principles are well understood and practiced. They conduct an annual engagement survey that addresses, among other things, the quality and effectiveness of BlackRock's HR and talent practices. And they played central roles in helping Fink, the GEC, and the HCC roll out the We Are One BlackRock and guiding-principles workshops. Two of the principles capture the firm's capacity to manage this tension: "We are a fiduciary to our clients" (enduring) and "We are innovators" (regenerative). Little is left to chance at BlackRock: Its executives are committed to measuring everything—talent management, development programs, engagement, rewards, and reputation. Hay Group, which performs global engagement studies, has recently included BlackRock in its high-performance norm group.

Game-changing companies build three winning capabilities simultaneously: They are purpose-driven, performance-oriented, and principles-led. We believe that their secret weapon is superior talent strategies characterized by deep commitment from the top executive team, broad-based engagement, and line accountability, with a "leaders developing leaders" culture.

These talent strategies are completely aligned with the companies' enterprise and business strategies; they are transparent and authentic; and they are guided by skilled professionals who know that superior talent can be crafted only by mastering the complexities and tensions of a postglobalization age. They are globally scaled yet locally relevant. They engender a sense of collective passion and purpose while enabling high potentials to thrive as individuals. And finally, they maintain that hunger for revitalization and renewal that is the hallmark of a game-changing company.

Originally published in January–February 2014. Reprint R1401D

Your Approach to Hiring Is All Wrong

by Peter Cappelli

BUSINESSES HAVE NEVER done as much hiring as they do today. They've never spent as much money doing it. And they've never done a worse job of it.

For most of the post–World War II era, large corporations went about hiring this way: Human resources experts prepared a detailed *job analysis* to determine what tasks the job required and what attributes a good candidate should have. Next they did a *job evaluation* to determine how the job fit into the organizational chart and how much it should pay, especially compared with other jobs. Ads were posted, and applicants applied. Then came the task of sorting through the applicants. That included skills tests, reference checks, maybe personality and IQ tests, and extensive interviews to learn more about them as people. William H. Whyte, in *The Organization Man*, described this process as going on for as long as a week before the winning candidate was offered the job. The vast majority of non-entry-level openings were filled from within.

Today's approach couldn't be more different. Census data shows, for example, that the majority of people who took a new job last year weren't searching for one: Somebody came and got them. Companies seek to fill their recruiting funnel with as many candidates as possible, especially "passive candidates," who aren't looking to move. Often employers advertise jobs that don't exist, hoping to find people who might be useful later on or in a different context.

The recruiting and hiring function has been eviscerated. Many U.S. companies—about 40%, according to research by Korn Ferry—have outsourced much if not all of the hiring process to "recruitment process outsourcers," which in turn use subcontractors, typically in India and the Philippines. The subcontractors scour LinkedIn and social media to find potential candidates. They sometimes contact them directly to see whether they can be persuaded to apply for a position and negotiate the salary they're willing to accept. (The recruiters get incentive pay if they negotiate the amount down.) To hire programmers, for example, these subcontractors can scan websites that programmers might visit, trace their "digital exhaust" from cookies and other user-tracking measures to identify who they are, and then examine their curricula vitae.

At companies that still do their own recruitment and hiring, managers trying to fill open positions are largely left to figure out what the jobs require and what the ads should say. When applications come—always electronically—applicant-tracking software sifts through them for key words that the hiring managers want to see. Then the process moves into the Wild West, where a new industry of vendors offers an astonishing array of smart-sounding tools that claim to predict who will be a good hire. They use voice recognition, body language, clues on social media, and especially machine learning algorithms—everything but tea leaves. Entire publications are devoted to what these vendors are doing.

The big problem with all these new practices is that we don't know whether they actually produce satisfactory hires. Only about a third of U.S. companies report that they monitor whether their hiring practices lead to good employees; few of them do so carefully, and only a minority even track cost per hire and time to hire. Imagine if the CEO asked how an advertising campaign had gone, and the response was "We have a good idea how long it took to roll out and what it cost, but we haven't looked to see whether we're selling more."

Hiring talent remains the number one concern of CEOs in the most recent Conference Board Annual Survey; it's also the top concern of the entire executive suite. PwC's 2017 CEO survey reports that chief executives view the unavailability of talent and skills as the biggest

Idea in Brief

The Problem

Employers continue to hire at a high rate and spend enormous sums to do it. But they don't know whether their approaches are effective at finding and selecting good candidates.

The Root Causes

Businesses focus on external candidates and don't track the results of their approaches. They often use outside vendors and high-tech tools that are unproven and have inherent flaws.

The Solution

Return to filling most positions by promoting from within. Measure the results produced by vendors and new tools, and be on the lookout for discrimination and privacy violations.

threat to their business. Employers also spend an enormous amount on hiring—an average of $4,129 per job in the United States, according to Society for Human Resource Management estimates, and many times that amount for managerial roles—and the United States fills a staggering 66 million jobs a year. Most of the $20 billion that companies spend on human resources vendors goes to hiring.

Why do employers spend so much on something so important while knowing so little about whether it works?

Where the Problem Starts

Survey after survey finds employers complaining about how difficult hiring is. There may be many explanations, such as their having become very picky about candidates, especially in the slack labor market of the Great Recession. But clearly they are hiring much more than at any other time in modern history, for two reasons.

The first is that openings are now filled more often by hiring from the outside than by promoting from within. In the era of lifetime employment, from the end of World War II through the 1970s, corporations filled roughly 90% of their vacancies through promotions and lateral assignments. Today the figure is a third or less. When they hire from outside, organizations don't have to pay to train and develop their employees. Since the restructuring waves of the early 1980s, it has been relatively easy to find experienced talent outside. Only 28% of talent acquisition leaders today report that internal candidates are an important source of people to fill vacancies—presumably because of less internal development and fewer clear career ladders.

Less promotion internally means that hiring efforts are no longer concentrated on entry-level jobs and recent graduates. (If you doubt this, go to the "careers" link on any company website and look for a job opening that doesn't require prior experience.) Now companies must be good at hiring across most levels, because the candidates they want are already doing the job somewhere else. These people don't need training, so they may be ready to contribute right away, but they are much harder to find.

The second reason hiring is so difficult is that retention has become tough: Companies hire from their competitors and vice versa, so they have to keep replacing people who leave. Census and Bureau of Labor Statistics data shows that 95% of hiring is done to fill existing positions. Most of those vacancies are caused by voluntary turnover. LinkedIn data indicates that the most common reason employees consider a position elsewhere is career advancement—which is surely related to employers' not promoting to fill vacancies.

The root cause of most hiring, therefore, is drastically poor retention. Here are some simple ways to fix that:

Track the percentage of openings filled from within

An adage of business is that we manage what we measure, but companies don't seem to be applying that maxim to tracking hires. Most are shocked to learn how few of their openings are filled from within—is it really the case that their people can't handle different and bigger roles?

Require that all openings be posted internally

Internal job boards were created during the dot-com boom to reduce turnover by making it easier for people to find new jobs within their existing employer. Managers weren't even allowed to know if a subordinate was looking to move within the company, for fear that they would try to block that person and he or she would leave. But during the Great Recession employees weren't quitting, and many companies slid back to the old model whereby managers could prevent their subordinates from moving internally. J. R. Keller, of Cornell University, has found that when managers could fill a vacancy with someone they already had in mind, they ended up with employees who performed more poorly than those hired when the job had been posted and anyone could apply. The commonsense explanation for this is that few enterprises really know what talent and capabilities they have.

Recognize the costs of outside hiring

In addition to the time and effort of hiring, my colleague Matthew Bidwell found, outside hires take three years to perform as well as internal hires in the same job, while internal hires take seven years to earn as much as outside hires are paid. Outside hiring also causes current employees to spend time and energy positioning themselves for jobs elsewhere. It disrupts the culture and burdens peers who must help new hires figure out how things work.

None of this is to suggest that outside hiring is necessarily a bad idea. But unless your company is a Silicon Valley gazelle, adding new jobs at a furious pace, you should ask yourself some serious questions if most of your openings are being filled from outside.

A different approach for dealing with retention (which seems creepy to some) is to try to determine who is interested in leaving and then intervene. Vendors like Jobvite comb social media and public sites for clues, such as LinkedIn profile updates. Measuring "flight risk" is one of the most common goals of companies that do their own sophisticated HR analytics. This is reminiscent of the early days of job boards, when employers would try to find out who was posting résumés and either punish them or embrace them, depending on leadership's mood.

Whether companies should be examining social media content in relation to hiring or any other employment action is a challenging ethical question. On one hand, the information is essentially public and may reveal relevant information. On the other hand, it is

Protecting Against Discrimination

Finding out whether your practices result in good hires is not only basic to good management but the only real defense against claims of adverse impact and discrimination. Other than white males under age 40 with no disabilities or work-related health problems, workers have special protections under federal and state laws against hiring practices that may have an adverse impact on them. As a practical matter, that means if members of a particular group are less likely to be recruited or hired, the employer must show that the hiring process is not discriminatory.

The only defense against evidence of adverse impact is for the employer to show that its hiring practices are valid—that is, they predict who will be a good employee in meaningful and statistically significant ways—and that no alternative would predict as well with less adverse impact. That analysis must be conducted with data on the employer's own applicants and hires. The fact that the vendor that sold you the test you use has evidence that it was valid in other contexts is not sufficient.

---

invasive, and candidates are rarely asked for permission to scrutinize their information. Hiring a private detective to shadow a candidate would also gather public information that might be relevant, yet most people would view it as an unacceptable invasion of privacy.

The Hiring Process

When we turn to hiring itself, we find that employers are missing the forest for the trees: Obsessed with new technologies and driving down costs, they largely ignore the ultimate goal: making the best possible hires. Here's how the process should be revamped:

Don't post "phantom jobs"

It costs nothing to post job openings on a company website, which are then scooped up by Indeed and other online companies and pushed out to potential job seekers around the world. Thus it may be unsurprising that some of these jobs don't really exist. Employers may simply be fishing for candidates. ("Let's see if someone really great is out there, and if so, we'll create a position for him or her.") Often job ads stay up even after positions have been filled, to keep collecting candidates for future vacancies or just because it takes more effort to pull the ad down than to leave it up. Sometimes ads are posted by unscrupulous recruiters looking for résumés to pitch to clients elsewhere. Because these phantom jobs make the labor market look tighter than it really is, they are a problem for economic policy makers as well as for frustrated job seekers. Companies should take ads down when jobs are filled.

Design jobs with realistic requirements

Figuring out what the requirements of a job should be—and the corresponding attributes candidates must have—is a bigger challenge now, because so many companies have reduced the number of internal recruiters whose function, in part, is to push back on hiring managers' wish lists. ("That job doesn't require 10 years of experience," or "No one with all those qualifications will be willing to accept the salary you're proposing to pay.") My earlier research found that companies piled on job requirements, baked them into the applicant-tracking software that sorted résumés according to binary decisions (yes, it has the key word; no, it doesn't), and then found that virtually no applicants met all the criteria. Trimming recruiters, who have expertise in hiring, and handing the process over to hiring managers is a prime example of being penny-wise and pound-foolish.

Reconsider your focus on passive candidates

The recruiting process begins with a search for experienced people who aren't looking to move. This is based on the notion that something may be wrong with anyone who wants to leave his or her current job. (Of the more than 20,000 talent professionals who responded to a LinkedIn survey in 2015, 86% said their recruiting organizations focused "very much so" or "to some extent" on passive candidates; I suspect that if anything, that number has since grown.) Recruiters know that the vast majority of people are open to moving at the right price: Surveys of employees find that only about 15% are *not* open to moving. As the economist Harold Demsetz said when asked by a competing university if he was happy working where he was: "Make me unhappy."

Fascinating evidence from the LinkedIn survey cited above shows that although self-identified "passive" job seekers are different from "active" job seekers, it's not in the way we might think. The number one factor that would encourage the former to move is more money. For active candidates the top factor is better work and career opportunities. More active than passive job seekers report that they are passionate about their work, engaged in improving their skills, and reasonably satisfied with their current jobs. They seem interested in moving because they are ambitious, not because they want higher pay.

Employers spend a vastly disproportionate amount of their budgets on recruiters who chase passive candidates, but on average they fill only 11% of their positions with individually targeted people, according to research by Gerry Crispin and Chris Hoyt, of CareerXroads. I know of no evidence that passive candidates become better employees, let alone that the process is cost-effective. If you focus on passive candidates, think carefully about what that actually gets you. Better yet, check your data to find out.

Understand the limits of referrals

The most popular channel for finding new hires is through employee referrals; up to 48% come from them, according to LinkedIn research. It seems like a cheap way to go, but does it produce better hires? Many employers think so. It's hard to know whether that's true, however, given that they don't check. And research by Emilio Castilla and colleagues suggests otherwise: They find that when referrals work out better than other hires, it's because their referrers look after them and essentially onboard them. If a referrer leaves before the new hire begins, the latter's performance is no better than that of nonreferrals, which is why it makes sense to pay referral bonuses six months or so after the person is hired—if he or she is still there.

A downside to referrals, of course, is that they can lead to a homogeneous workforce, because the people we know tend to be like us. This matters greatly for organizations interested in diversity, since recruiting is the only avenue allowed under U.S. law to increase diversity in a workforce. The Supreme Court has ruled that demographic criteria cannot be used even to break ties among candidates.

Measure the results

Few employers know which channel produces the best candidates at the lowest cost because they don't track the outcomes. Tata is an exception: It has long done what I advocate. For college recruiting, for example, it calculates which schools send it employees who perform the best, stay the longest, and are paid the lowest starting wage. Other employers should follow suit and monitor recruiting channels and employees' performance to identify which sources produce the best results.

Persuade fewer people to apply

The hiring industry pays a great deal of attention to "the funnel," whereby readers of a company's job postings become applicants, are interviewed, and ultimately are offered jobs. Contrary to the popular belief that the U.S. job market is extremely tight right now, most jobs still get lots of applicants. Recruiting and hiring consultants and vendors estimate that about 2% of applicants receive offers. Unfortunately, the main effort to improve hiring—virtually always aimed at making it faster and cheaper—has been to shovel more applicants into the funnel. Employers do that primarily through marketing, trying to get out the word that they are great places to work. Whether doing this is a misguided way of trying to attract better hires or just meant to make the organization feel more desirable isn't clear.

Much better to go in the other direction: Create a smaller but better-qualified applicant pool to improve the yield. Here's why: Every applicant costs you money—especially now, in a labor market where applicants have started to "ghost" employers, abandoning their applications midway through the process. Every application also exposes a company to legal risk, because the company has obligations to candidates (not to discriminate, for example) just as it does to employees. And collecting lots of applicants in a wide funnel means that a great many of them won't fit the job or the company, so employers have to rely on the next step of the hiring process—selection—to weed them out. As we will see, employers aren't good at that.

FIGURE 2-1

The grass is always greener . . .

Organizations are much more interested in external talent than in their own employees to fill vacancies.

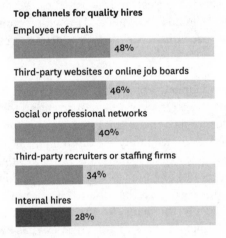

Top channels for quality hires

Employee referrals
48%

Third-party websites or online job boards
46%

Social or professional networks
40%

Third-party recruiters or staffing firms
34%

Internal hires
28%

Source: LinkedIn, based on a 2017 survey of 3,973 talent-acquisition decision makers who work in corporate HR departments and are LinkedIn members.

Once people are candidates, they may not be completely honest about their skills or interests—because they want to be hired—and employers' ability to find out the truth is limited. More than a generation ago the psychologist John Wanous proposed giving applicants a realistic preview of what the job is like. That still makes sense as a way to head off those who would end up being unhappy in the job. It's not surprising that Google has found a way to do this with gamification: Job seekers see what the work would be like by playing a game version of it. Marriott has done the same, even for low-level employees. Its My Marriott Hotel game targets young people in developing countries who may have had little experience in hotels to show them what it's like and to steer them to the recruiting site if they score well on the game. The key for any company, though, is that the preview should make clear what is difficult and challenging about the work as well as why it's fun so that candidates who don't fit won't apply.

It should be easy for candidates to learn about a company and a job, but making it really easy to apply, just to fill up that funnel, doesn't make much sense. During the dot-com boom Texas Instruments cleverly introduced a preemployment test that allowed applicants to see their scores before they applied. If their scores weren't high enough for the company to take their applications seriously, they tended not to proceed, and the company saved the cost of having to process their applications.

If the goal is to get better hires in a cost-effective manner, it's more important to scare away candidates who don't fit than to jam more candidates into the recruiting funnel.

Test candidates' standard skills

How to determine which candidates to hire—what predicts who will be a good employee—has been rigorously studied at least since World War I. The personnel psychologists who investigated this have learned much about predicting good hires that contemporary organizations have since forgotten, such as that neither college grades nor unstructured sequential interviews (hopping from office to office) are a good predictor, whereas past performance is.

Since it can be difficult (if not impossible) to glean sufficient information about an outside applicant's past performance, what other predictors are good? There is remarkably little consensus even among experts. That's mainly because a typical job can have so many tasks and aspects, and different factors predict success at different tasks.

There is general agreement, however, that testing to see whether individuals have standard skills is about the best we can do. Can the candidate speak French? Can she do simple programming tasks? And so forth. But just doing the tests is not enough. The economists Mitchell Hoffman, Lisa B. Kahn, and Danielle Li found that even when companies conduct such tests, hiring managers often ignore them—and when they do, they get worse hires. The psychologist Nathan Kuncel and colleagues discovered that even when hiring managers use objective criteria and tests, applying their own weights and judgment to those criteria leads them to pick worse candidates than if they had used a standard formula. Only 40% of employers, however, do any tests of skills or general abilities, including IQ. What are they doing instead? Seventy-four percent do drug tests, including for marijuana use; even employers in states where recreational use is now legal still seem to do so.

Be wary of vendors bearing high-tech gifts

Into the testing void has come a new group of entrepreneurs who either are data scientists or have them in tow. They bring a fresh approach to the hiring process—but often with little understanding of how hiring actually works. John Sumser, of HRExaminer, an online newsletter that focuses on HR technology, estimates that on average, companies get five to seven pitches *every day*—almost all of them about hiring—from vendors using data science to address HR issues. These vendors have all sorts of cool-sounding assessments, such as computer games that can be scored to predict who will be a good hire. We don't know whether any of these actually lead to better hires, because few of them are validated against actual job performance. That aside, these assessments have spawned a counterwave of vendors who help candidates learn how to score well on them. Lloyds Bank, for example, developed a virtual-reality-based assessment of candidate potential, and JobTestPrep offers to teach potential candidates how to do well on it. Especially for IT and technical jobs, cheating on skills tests and even video interviews (where colleagues off camera give help) is such a concern that eTeki and other specialized vendors help employers figure out who is cheating in real time.

Revamp your interviewing process

The amount of time employers spend on interviews has almost doubled since 2009, according to research from Glassdoor. How much of that increase represents delays in setting up those interviews is impossible to tell, but it provides at least a partial explanation for why it takes longer to fill jobs now. Interviews are arguably the most difficult technique to get right, because interviewers should stick to questions that predict good hires—mainly about past behavior or performance that's relevant to the tasks of the job—and ask them consistently across candidates. Just winging it and asking whatever comes to mind is next to useless.

More important, interviews are where biases most easily show up, because interviewers do usually decide on the fly what to ask of whom and how to interpret the answer. Everyone knows some executive who is absolutely certain he knows the one question that will really predict good candidates ("If you were stranded on a desert island. . ."). The sociologist Lauren Rivera's examination of interviews for elite positions, such as those in professional services firms, indicates that hobbies, particularly those associated with the rich, feature prominently as a selection criterion.

Interviews are most important for assessing "fit with our culture," which is the number one hiring criterion employers report using, according to research from the Rockefeller Foundation. It's also one of the squishiest attributes to measure, because few organizations have an accurate and consistent view of their own culture—and even if they do, understanding what attributes represent a good fit is not straightforward. For example, does the fact that an applicant belonged to a fraternity reflect experience working with others or elitism or bad attitudes toward women? Should it be completely irrelevant? Letting someone with no experience or training make such calls is a recipe for bad hires and, of course, discriminatory behavior. Think hard about whether your interviewing protocols make any sense and resist the urge to bring even more managers into the interview process.

Recognize the strengths and weaknesses of machine learning models

Culture fit is another area into which new vendors are swarming. Typically they collect data from current employees, create a machine learning model to predict the attributes of the best ones, and then use that model to hire candidates with the same attributes.

As with many other things in this new industry, that sounds good until you think about it; then it becomes replete with problems. Given the best performers of the past, the algorithm will almost certainly include *white* and *male* as key variables. If it's restricted from using that category, it will come up with attributes associated with being a white male, such as playing rugby.

Machine learning models do have the potential to find important but previously unconsidered relationships. Psychologists, who have dominated research on hiring, have been keen to study attributes relevant to their interests, such as personality, rather than asking the broader question "What identifies a potential good hire?" Their results gloss over the fact that they often have only a trivial ability to predict who will be a good performer, particularly when many factors are involved. Machine learning, in contrast, can come up with highly predictive factors. Research by Evolv, a workforce analytics pioneer (now part of Cornerstone OnDemand), found that expected commuting distance for the candidate predicted turnover very well. But that's not a question the psychological models thought to ask. (And even that question has problems.)

The advice on selection is straightforward: Test for skills. Ask assessments vendors to show evidence that they can actually predict who the good employees will be. Do fewer, more-consistent interviews.

Originally published in May–June 2019. Reprint R1903B

"A Players" or "A Positions"?

The Strategic Logic of Workforce Management.

by Mark A. Huselid, Richard W. Beatty, and Brian E. Becker

A GREAT WORKFORCE IS made up of great people. What could be more intuitively obvious? Is it any wonder, then, that so many companies have devoted so much energy in recent years to identifying, developing, and retaining what have come to be known as "A players"? Firms like GE, IBM, and Microsoft all have well-developed systems for managing and motivating their high-performance and high-potential employees—and for getting rid of their mediocre ones. Management thinkers have widely endorsed this approach: Larry Bossidy, in the best-selling book *Execution,* for example, calls this sort of differentiation among employees "the mother's milk of building a performance culture."

But focusing exclusively on A players puts, well, the horse before the cart. High performers aren't going to add much value to an organization if they're smoothly and rapidly pulling carts that aren't going to market. They're going to be effective only when they're harnessed to the right cart—that is, engaged in work that's essential to company strategy. This, too, may seem obvious. But it's surprising how few companies systematically identify their strategically important A *positions*—and *then* focus on the A players who should fill them. Even fewer companies manage their A positions in such a way that the A players are able to deliver the A performance needed in these crucial roles.

While conventional wisdom might argue that the firms with the most talent win, we believe that, given the financial and managerial resources needed to attract, select, develop, and retain high performers, companies simply can't afford to have A players in all positions. Rather, we believe that the firms with the *right* talent win. Businesses need to adopt a portfolio approach to workforce management, placing the very best employees in strategic positions, good performers in support positions, and eliminating nonperforming employees and jobs that don't add value.

We offer here a method for doing just that, drawing on the experience of several companies that are successfully adopting this approach to workforce management, some of which we have worked with in our research or as consultants. One thing to keep in mind: Effective management of your A positions requires intelligent management of your B and C positions, as well.

Identifying Your A Positions

People traditionally have assessed the relative value of jobs in an organization in one of two ways. Human resource professionals typically focus on the level of skill, effort, and responsibility a job entails, together with working conditions. From this point of view, the most important positions are those held by the most highly skilled, hardest-working employees, exercising the most responsibility and operating in the most challenging environments.

Economists, by contrast, generally believe that people's wages reflect the value they create for the company and the relative scarcity of their skills in the labor market. Thus, the most important jobs are those held by the most highly paid employees. The trouble with both of these approaches is that they merely identify which jobs the company is currently treating as most important, not the ones that actually are. To do that, one must not work backward from organization charts or compensation systems but forward from strategy.

That's why we believe the two defining characteristics of an A position are first, as you might expect, its disproportionate importance to a company's ability to execute some part of its strategy and

Idea in Brief

Superior talent gives your company its competitive edge. But your star performers can't burnish your bottom line unless you deploy them in those few jobs through which you execute your high-level strategy. If you haven't identified those "A positions," you may be drastically mismanaging your workforce—rewarding high performers in non-strategic jobs, or keeping B or even C players in mission-critical roles.

How to take a more disciplined approach to workforce management? Identify your A positions—those most essential to your strategy. Probably less than 20% of your jobs, A positions are likely scattered throughout your organization, at all levels. Then actively develop and generously compensate the high performers in those roles. Move C players out of A positions, replacing them with top talent. Help B players in strategic positions to elevate their performance to A level.

No company can afford to have A players in all positions. But by placing your very best people in strategic positions, investing disproportionately in them, and managing your B and C players shrewdly, you create a workforce that can carry out your strategy—and leave rivals scrambling.

second—and this is not nearly as obvious—the wide variability in the quality of the work displayed among the employees in the position.

Plainly, then, to determine a position's strategic significance, you must be clear about your company's strategy: Do you compete on the basis of price? On quality? Through mass customization? Then you need to identify your strategic capabilities—the technologies, information, and skills required to create the intended competitive advantage. Walmart's low-cost strategy, for instance, requires state-of-the-art logistics, information systems, and a relentless managerial focus on efficiency and cost reduction. Finally, you must ask: What jobs are critical to employing those capabilities in the execution of the strategy?

Such positions are as variable as the strategies they promote. Consider the retailers Nordstrom and Costco. Both rely on customer satisfaction to drive growth and shareholder value, but what different forms that satisfaction takes: At Nordstrom it involves personalized service and advice, whereas at Costco low prices and product

Idea in Practice

To manage your workforce strategically:

Identify Your A Positions

A positions are crucial to your company's ability to execute some part of its strategy. To identify these positions, clarify the basis on which your company competes: Price? Quality? Mass customization? Then identify the technologies, information, and skills required to create your intended competitive advantage. Ask which jobs employ those critical capabilities in the execution of your strategy.

Example:

- Nordstrom and Costco both rely on customer satisfaction to drive growth and shareholder value. But Nordstrom's strategy hinges on personalized service and advice, while Costco's relies on low prices and product availability. Nordstrom's A positions therefore include frontline sales associate jobs, while Costco's includes purchasing manager roles.

Manage Your A Positions

Manage your A positions using these techniques:

- **Evaluation.** Determine what differentiates high and low performance in each A position. Measure people against those criteria.

Example:

- At IBM, A positions include deal-making roles—where people assemble sets of products, software, and expertise that particular clients need. IBM identified 10 attributes (including ability to partner with clients) critical to these positions. It measures each attribute on a four-point scale delineated with behavioral benchmarks. Employees in those roles assess themselves on these attributes and are assessed through 360-degree feedback.

- **Development.** Actively develop people in A positions by providing training and professional development opportunities.

availability are key. So the jobs critical to creating strategic advantage at the two companies will be different. Frontline sales associates are vital to Nordstrom but hardly to be found at Costco, where purchasing managers are absolutely central to success.

Example:

- More than $450 million of the $750 million IBM spends annually on employee development goes to people in A positions. IBM requires them to define development programs for themselves. These programs are based on strengths and weaknesses revealed in performance evaluations and draw on intranet tools designed to improve performance on each attribute.

- **Compensation.** Generously compensate A players in A positions. At IBM, annual salary increases go to only half the workforce. Top-performing employees get raises roughly three times higher than simply strong performers.

- **Succession.** Build bench strength for each A position.

IBM invests heavily in feeder jobs for A positions. It regularly assesses feeder employees' readiness for promotion into strategically important roles. It also identifies "pass-through" jobs where people can develop needed skills, and fills these jobs with A-position candidates.

Manage Your Workforce Portfolio

Intelligently managing your A positions isn't enough: Manage B and C positions, too. B positions can support A positions (think IBM's feeder roles). Consider outsourcing or eliminating C jobs. At minimum, move C players out of A positions and help B players in those roles become A players.

The point is, there are no inherently strategic positions. Furthermore, they're relatively rare—less than 20% of the workforce—and are likely to be scattered around the organization. They could include the biochemist in R&D or the field sales representative in marketing.

So far, our argument is straightforward. But why would variability in the performance of the people currently in a job be so important? Because, as in other portfolios, variation in job performance represents upside potential—raising the average performance of individuals in these critical roles will pay huge dividends in corporate value. Furthermore, if that variance exists across companies, it may also be a source of competitive advantage for a particular firm, making the position strategically important.

Sales positions, fundamental to the success of many a company's strategy, are a good case in point: A salesperson whose performance is in the 85th percentile of a company's sales staff frequently generates five to 10 times the revenue of someone in the 50th percentile. But we're not just talking about greater or lesser value creation—we're also talking about the potential for value creation versus value destruction. The Gallup organization, for instance, surveyed 45,000 customers of a company known for customer service to evaluate its 4,600 customer service representatives. The reps' performance ranged widely: The top quartile of workers had a positive effect on 61% of the customers they talked to, the second quartile had a positive effect on only 40%, the third quartile had a positive effect on just 27%—and the bottom quartile actually had, as a group, a negative effect on customers. These people—at the not insignificant cost to the company of roughly $40 million a year (assuming average total compensation of $35,000 per person)—were collectively destroying value by alienating customers and, presumably, driving many of them away.

Although the $40 million in wasted resources is jaw-dropping, the real significance of this situation is the huge difference that replacing or improving the performance of the subpar reps would make. If managers focused disproportionately on this position, whether through intensive training or more careful screening of the people hired for it, company performance would improve tremendously.

The strategic job that doesn't display a great deal of variability in performance is relatively rare, even for those considered entry-level. That's because performance in these jobs involves more than proficiency in carrying out a task. Consider the job of cashier. The generic mechanics aren't difficult. But if the position is part of a retail strategy emphasizing the customers' buying experience, the job will certainly involve more than scanning products and collecting money with a friendly smile. Cashiers might, for example, be required to take a look at what a customer is buying and then suggest other products that the person might want to consider on a return visit. In such cases, there is likely to be a wide range in people's performance.

Some jobs may exhibit high levels of variability (the sales staff on the floor at a big-box store like Costco, for example) but have little strategic impact (because, as we have noted, Costco's strategy does not depend on sales staff to ensure customer satisfaction). Neither dramatically improving the overall level of performance in these jobs nor narrowing the variance would present an opportunity for improving competitive advantage.

Alternatively, some jobs may be potentially important strategically but currently represent little opportunity for competitive advantage since everyone's performance is already at a high level. That may either be because of the standardized nature of the job or because a company or industry has, through training or careful hiring, reduced the variability and increased the mean performance of workers to a point where further investment isn't merited. A pilot, for example, is a key contributor to most airlines' strategic goal of safety, but owing to regular training throughout pilots' careers and government regulations, most pilots perform well. Although there definitely is a strategic downside if the performance of some pilots were to fall into the unsafe category, improving pilot performance in the area of safety is unlikely and, even if marginal gains are possible, unlikely to provide an opportunity for competitive advantage.

So a job must meet the dual criteria of strategic impact and performance variability if it is to qualify as an A position. From these two defining characteristics flow a number of others—for example, a position's potential to substantially increase revenue or reduce costs—that mark an A position and distinguish it from B and C positions. B positions are those that are either indirectly strategic through their support of A positions or are potentially strategic but currently exhibit little performance variability and therefore offer

TABLE 3-1

Which jobs make the most difference?

An A position is defined primarily by its impact on strategy and by the range in the performance level of the people in the position. From these two characteristics flow a number of other attributes that distinguish A positions from B and C jobs.

	A Position STRATEGIC	B Position SUPPORT	C Position SURPLUS
DEFINING CHARACTERISTICS	Has a direct strategic impact AND Exhibits high performance variability among those in the position, representing upside potential	Has an indirect strategic impact by supporting strategic positions and minimizes downside risk by providing a foundation for strategic efforts OR Has a potential strategic impact, but exhibits little performance variability among those in the position	May be required for the firm to function but has little strategic impact
SCOPE OF AUTHORITY	Autonomous decision-making	Specific processes or procedures typically must be followed	Little discretion in work
PRIMARY DETERMINANT OF COMPENSATION	Performance	Job level	Market price
EFFECT ON VALUE CREATION	Creates value by substantially enhancing revenue or reducing costs	Supports value-creating positions	Has little positive economic impact
CONSEQUENCES OF MISTAKES	May be very costly, but missed revenue opportunities are a greater loss to the firm	May be very costly and can destroy value	Not necessarily costly
CONSEQUENCES OF HIRING WRONG PERSON	Significant expense in terms of lost training investment and revenue opportunities	Fairly easily remedied through hiring of replacement	Easily remedied through hiring of replacement

little opportunity for competitive advantage. Although B positions are unlikely to create value, they are often important in maintaining it. C positions are those that play no role in furthering a company's strategy, have little effect on the creation or maintenance of value—and may, in fact, not be needed at all. (For a comparison of some attributes of these three types of positions, see the exhibit "Which jobs make the most difference?")

It's important to emphasize that A positions have nothing to do with a firm's hierarchy—which is the criterion executive teams so often use to identify their organizations' critical and opportunity-rich roles. As natural as it may be for you, as a senior executive, to view your own job as among a select group of vital positions in the company, resist this temptation. As we saw in the case of the cashier, A positions can be found throughout an organization and may be relatively simple jobs that nonetheless need to be performed creatively and in ways that fit and further a company's unique strategy.

A big pharmaceutical firm, for instance, trying to pinpoint the jobs that have a high impact on the company's success, identifies several A positions. Because its ability to test the safety and efficacy of its products is a required strategic capability, the head of clinical trials, as well as a number of positions in the regulatory affairs office, are deemed critical. But some top jobs in the company hierarchy, including the director of manufacturing and the corporate treasurer, are not. Although people in these jobs are highly compensated, make important decisions, and play key roles in maintaining the company's value, they don't *create* value through the firm's business model. Consequently, the company chooses not to make the substantial investments (in, say, succession planning) in these positions that it does for more strategic jobs.

A positions also aren't defined by how hard they are to fill, even though many managers mistakenly equate workforce scarcity with workforce value. A tough job to fill may not have that high potential to increase a firm's value. At a high-tech manufacturing company, for example, a quality assurance manager plays a crucial role in making certain that the products meet customers' expectations. The job requires skills that may be difficult to find. But, like the airline pilots, the position's impact on company success is asymmetrical. The downside may indeed be substantial: Quality that falls below Six Sigma levels will certainly destroy value for the company. But the upside is limited: A manager able to achieve a Nine Sigma defect rate won't add much value because the difference between Six Sigma and Nine Sigma won't be great enough to translate into any major value creation opportunity (although the difference between Two- and Three-Sigma defect rates may well be). Thus, while such a position could be hard to fill, it doesn't fit the definition of an A position.

Managing Your A Positions

Having identified your A positions, you'll need to manage them—both individually and as part of a portfolio of A, B, and C positions—so that they and the people in them in fact further your organization's strategic objectives.

A first and crucial step is to explain to your workforce clearly and explicitly the reasons that different jobs and people need to be treated differently. Pharmaceutical company GlaxoSmithKline is identifying those positions, at both the corporate and business-unit levels, that are critical to the company's success in a rapidly changing competitive environment. As part of that initiative, the company developed a statement of its workforce philosophy and management guidelines. One of these explicitly addresses "workforce differentiation" and reads, in part: "It is essential that we have key talent in critical positions and that the careers of these individuals are managed centrally."

But communication is just the beginning. A positions also require a disproportionate level of investment. The performance of people in these roles needs to be evaluated in detail, these individuals must be actively developed, and they need to be generously compensated. Also, a pipeline must be created to ensure that their successors are among the best people available. IBM is a company making aggressive investments on each of these four fronts.

In recent years, IBM has worked to develop what it calls an "on-demand workforce," made up of people who can quickly put together or become part of a package of hardware, software, and consulting services that will meet the specific needs of an individual customer. As part of this effort, IBM has sought to attract and retain certain individuals with what it terms the "hot skills" customers want in such bundled offerings.

In the past year or so, the company has also focused on identifying its A positions. The roster of such positions clearly will change as IBM's business does. But some, such as the country general manager, are likely to retain their disproportionate value. Other strategic roles include midlevel manager positions, dubbed "deal makers," responsible for the central strategic task of pulling together, from both inside and outside the company, the diverse set of products, software, and expertise that a particular client will find attractive.

Evaluation

Because of their importance, IBM's key positions are filled with top-notch people: Obviously, putting A players in these A positions helps to ensure A performance. But IBM goes further, taking steps to hold its A players to high standards through an explicit process—determining the factors that differentiate high and low performance in each position and then measuring people against those criteria. The company last year developed a series of 10 leadership attributes—such as the abilities to form partnerships with clients and to take strategic risks—each of which is measured on a four-point scale delineated with clear behavioral benchmarks. Individuals assess themselves on these attributes and are also assessed by others, using 360-degree feedback.

Development

Such detailed evaluation isn't very valuable unless it's backed up by a robust professional development system. Drawing on the strengths and weaknesses revealed in their evaluations and with the help of tools available on the company's intranet, people in IBM's A positions are required to put together a development program for themselves in each of the 10 leadership areas.

This is only one of numerous development opportunities offered to people in A positions. In fact, more than $450 million of the

$750 million that IBM spends annually on employee development is targeted at either fostering hot skills (both today's and those expected to be tomorrow's) or the development of people in key positions. A senior-level executive devotes all of his time to programs designed to develop the executive capabilities of people in these jobs.

Compensation

IBM supports this disproportionate investment in development with an even more disproportionate compensation system. Traditionally at IBM, even employees with low performance ratings had received regular salary increases and bonuses. Today, annual salary increases go to only about half the workforce, and the best-performing employees get raises roughly three times as high as those received by the simply strong performers.

Succession

Perhaps most important, IBM has worked to formalize succession planning and to build bench strength for each of its key positions, in part by investing heavily in feeder jobs for those roles. People in these feeder positions are regularly assessed to determine if they are "ready now," "one job away," or "two jobs away" from promotion into the strategically important roles. "Pass-through" jobs, in which people can develop needed skills, are identified and filled with candidates for the key strategic positions. For example, the position of regional sales manager is an important pass-through job on the way to becoming a country general manager. In this way, IBM ensures that its A people will in fact be ready to fill its top positions.

Managing Your Portfolio of Positions

Intelligently managing your A positions can't be done in isolation. You also need strategies for managing your B and C positions and an understanding of how all three strategies work together. We find it ironic that managers who embrace a portfolio approach in other areas of the business can be slow to apply this type of thinking to their workforce. All too frequently, for example, companies invest in their best and worst employees in equal measure. The unhappy

Are We Differentiating Enough?

Managers who know that differentiated strategies are the key to competitive success all too often fail to differentiate in strategies for their most important asset—their workforce. This checklist can help you determine if you are differentiating enough in the treatment of your company's positions and people. If you check off any of these, you have work to do.

Positions

- Position descriptions are based on history, not strategic value.
- Most positions are paid at about the market midpoint.
- Recruitment and retention for all positions involve the same effort and budget.
- The same selection process is used for all positions.
- Little developmental rotation occurs.
- Few C positions are eliminated or outsourced.

Players

- Performance evaluation forms are completed rarely or only at salary review.
- There is little candor in performance reviews.
- Many or most employees are rated the same.
- Forced distribution of ratings is used.
- Those receiving the middle rating are labeled "proficient" or "successful" and receive regular pay raises despite being viewed as average or marginal.
- Both very tough and very lenient raters operate without consequences.
- Poor performers stay yet don't improve.
- Top management is not rigorously evaluated.

result is often the departure of A players, discouraged by their treatment, and the retention of C players.

To say that you need to disproportionately invest in your A positions and players doesn't mean that you ignore the rest of your workforce. B positions are important either as support for A positions (as IBM's feeder positions are) or because of any potentially large downside implications of their roles (as with the airline pilots). Put another way, although you aren't likely to win with your B positions, you can certainly lose with them.

As for those nonstrategic C positions, you may conclude after careful analysis that, just as you need to weed out C players over time, you may need to weed out your C positions, by outsourcing or even eliminating the work.

Roche is one firm that is placing more emphasis on the strategic value of positions themselves. Over the past few years, the pharmaceutical company has been looking at different positions to determine which are necessary for maintaining competitive advantage. Regardless of how well a person performs in a role, if that position is no longer of strategic value, the job is eliminated. For example, Roche looked at the strategic value provided by data services in a recent project and as a result decided which positions needed to be added, which needed to change (or be moved)—and which, such as data center services (DCS) engineer, needed to be eliminated. In a similar manner, another pharmaceutical firm, Wyeth Consumer Healthcare, following a strategic decision to focus on large customers, eliminated what had been a strategic position for the company—middle-market account manager—as well as staff that supported the people in this position.

The ultimate aim is to manage your portfolio of positions so that the right people are in the right jobs, paying particular attention to your A positions. First, using performance criteria developed for determining who your A, B, and C players are, calculate the percentage of each currently in A positions. Then act quickly to get C players out of A positions, replace them with A players, and work to help B players in A positions become A players. GlaxoSmithKline currently is engaged in an initiative to push both line managers and HR staff to ensure that only top-tier employees (as determined by their performance evaluations) are in the company's identified key positions.

Making Tough Choices

Despite the obvious importance of developing high-performing employees and supporting the jobs that contribute most to company success, firms that routinely make difficult decisions about R&D, advertising, and manufacturing strategies rarely show the same discipline when it comes to their most valuable asset: the workforce. In fact, in our long experience, we've found that firms with the most highly differentiated R&D, product, and marketing strategies often have the most generic or undifferentiated workforce strategies. When a manager at one of these companies does make a tough choice in this area, the decision often relates to the costs rather than the value of the workforce. (The sidebar "Are we differentiating enough?" can help you determine whether you are making the distinctions likely to create workforce value.)

It would be nice to live in a world where we didn't have to make hard decisions about the workforce, but we don't. Strategy is about making choices, and correctly assessing employees and roles are two of the most important. For us, the essence of the issue is the distinction between equality and equity. Over the years, HR practices have evolved in a way that increasingly favors equal treatment of most employees within a given job. But today's competitive environment requires a shift from treating everyone the same to treating everyone according to his or her contribution.

We understand that this approach may not be for everyone, that increasing distinctions between employees and among jobs runs counter to some companies' cultures. There is, however, a psychological as well as a strategic benefit to an approach that initially focuses on A positions: Managers who are uncomfortable with the harsh A and C *player* distinction—especially those in HR, many of whom got into the business because they care about people—may find the idea of first differentiating between A and C *positions* more palatable. But shying away from making the more personal distinctions is also unwise. We all know that effective business strategy requires differentiating a firm's products and services in ways that create value for customers. Accomplishing this requires a differentiated workforce strategy, as well.

Originally published in December 2005. Reprint R0512G

Turning Potential into Success

The Missing Link in Leadership Development.

by Claudio Fernández-Aráoz, Andrew Roscoe, and Kentaro Aramaki

ORGANIZATIONS AROUND THE WORLD are failing on one key metric of success: leadership development. According to research from the Corporate Executive Board (CEB), 66% of companies invest in programs that aim to identify high-potential employees and help them advance, but only 24% of senior executives at those firms consider the programs to be a success. A mere 13% have confidence in the rising leaders at their firms, down from an already-low 17% just three years ago. And at the world's largest corporations—which each employ thousands of executives—a full 30% of new CEOs are hired from the outside.

The problem isn't a lack of internal talent. At Egon Zehnder we've been measuring executive potential for more than 30 years, and we've identified the predictors that correlate strongly with competence at the top. The first is *the right motivation*. This generally means a fierce commitment to excel in the pursuit of big, collective goals but, to a great extent, is contextual. For example, the leaders of a large charity and of an investment bank will need different kinds of motivation. This predictor can't easily be rated or compared meaningfully across individuals. However, the other predictors—*curiosity, insight, engagement,* and *determination*—can be measured and compared. And when we look at how managers in our global database (who come from thousands of companies in all sectors and are mostly in the top three levels of the hierarchy) score on those four key hallmarks, we find that 72% of them demonstrate the potential to grow into C-suite roles. In addition, 9% have what it takes to become competent CEOs.

Unfortunately, many organizations haven't figured out how to fully develop their prospective leaders. That limits these people's advancement and eventually their engagement and, ultimately, leads to turnover. Recent research from Gallup shows that 51% of U.S. managers feel disconnected from their jobs and companies, while 55% are looking for outside opportunities. And the problem cascades down: According to two comprehensive studies from Indeed. com, the most popular U.S. job-search website, 71% of employees are either actively hunting for or open to a new job, while 58% review postings at least monthly. The average rate of employee turnover (of which about three-quarters is voluntary) has been growing steadily for the past six years. In 2016 it hit a new high of 20.3% in the United States, and it's much higher in the most attractive sectors. The stats in other countries are comparable.

Low engagement and high turnover are extremely costly for organizations, especially if the people jumping ship are high potentials in whom much has already been invested. How can companies prevent this massive waste of talent and create more-effective development programs?

- First, by determining the most important competencies for leadership roles at their organizations. In our leadership advisory services at Egon Zehnder, we've identified seven that we believe are crucial for most executive positions at large companies: *results orientation, strategic orientation, collaboration and influence, team leadership, developing organizational capabilities, change leadership,* and *market understanding.* In addition, many leading companies are finding that an eighth— *inclusiveness*—is essential to executive performance.

- Second, by rigorously assessing the potential of aspiring managers: checking their motivational fit and carefully rating them on the four key hallmarks—curiosity, insight, engagement, and

Idea in Brief

The Problem

Corporate leadership development programs aren't working. Less than a quarter of executives at the organizations that have them think they're effective.

The Analysis

Evaluations of managers at thousands of corporations suggest that 72% have what it takes to grow into C-suite roles. How can we bridge the gap between this raw talent and executive success?

The Solution

By following four steps:

- Determine the most important competencies for leadership roles in your organization.

- Assess employees' potential by looking at the five predictors associated with success—motivation, curiosity, insight, engagement, and determination.

- Map people's potential to the competencies required in various roles.

- Give emerging leaders the opportunities, coaching, and support they need to strengthen the critical competencies.

determination. (See the June 2014 HBR article "21st-Century Talent Spotting" for a primer on this.)

- Third, by creating a growth map showing how a person's strengths in each of the hallmarks aligns with the competencies required in various roles.

- Fourth, by giving high potentials the right development opportunities—including job rotations and promotions they might not seem completely qualified for but that fit their growth maps—as well as targeted coaching and support.

Companies like Japan Tobacco and Prudential PLC, the British multinational life insurance and financial services group, have used this approach to enhance their talent development programs and boost their internal leadership pipelines. Following it requires deep commitment from senior executives and some investment in the human resources function. But the cost of inaction is greater: As competition for smart and able managers heats up around the world, organizations can't keep ignoring and demoralizing internal talent while filling their C-suites with expensive external hires. They must learn to grow their own leaders.

Getting a Read on Needs and Skills

Before an organization can begin mapping managers' potential to required competencies, it must determine what exactly it needs. That will vary from business to business. A company recently acquired by a private equity firm would probably want to make results orientation a priority, while the management of an old-fashioned bank trying to stay relevant in a digital age might need keen market understanding and a strategic orientation.

Requirements will vary from role to role within firms as well. Let's consider the competencies that the board of one pharmaceutical company we worked with projected that its CEO, CFO (who was also the chief strategy officer), and business unit heads would need three years down the road, given its midterm strategy. Like all chief executives, the CEO had to have strong strategic and results orientations. But this particular company was trying to adapt to the digital era and to become more diverse in its people and more flexible in its way of working, so the board also highlighted inclusiveness and team and change leadership as priorities. For the CFO—who would be tasked with overseeing the implementation of the new strategies—collaboration and influence, change leadership, and strategic orientation were deemed must-haves. And for the unit heads, who would be on the front lines of strategic and cultural change and also responsible for hitting demanding budgets, the key competencies were results orientation, developing organizational capabilities, team leadership, and inclusiveness.

Your organization should similarly aim to identify the competencies that are most crucial for its top roles in light of its own challenges and goals. We suggest rating the level of proficiency needed in each competency for each role on a scale from 1 to 7. (For a more detailed explanation of how to translate skill levels into numerical

TABLE 4-1

Levels of competence

We evaluate executives on their mastery of eight leadership competencies (listed in the far left column), assessing where they fall on a spectrum from 1 (baseline) to 7 (extraordinary). We have found that four traits—curiosity, insight, engagement, and determination—predict how far managers will progress. Below each competency are the traits linked to strength in it.

	1	2	3	4	5	6	7
RESULTS ORIENTATION, PREDICTED BY • DETERMINATION • CURIOSITY	Completes assignments	Works to make things better	Achieves goals	Exceeds goals	Improves firm's practices and performance	Redesigns practices for breakthrough results	Transforms business model
STRATEGIC ORIENTATION, PREDICTED BY • INSIGHT • CURIOSITY	Understands immediate issue	Defines plan within larger strategy	Sets multiyear priorities	Defines multi-year strategy for own area	Changes business strategy in multiple areas	Creates high-impact corporate strategy	Develops breakthrough corporate strategy
COLLABORATION AND INFLUENCE, PREDICTED BY • ENGAGEMENT • DETERMINATION • CURIOSITY	Responds to requests	Supports colleagues	Actively engages with colleagues	Motivates others to work with self	Facilitates cross-group collaboration	Establishes collaborative culture	Forges trans-formational partnerships
TEAM LEADERSHIP, PREDICTED BY • ENGAGEMENT • CURIOSITY	Directs work	Explains what to do and why	Gets input from team	Inspires team commitment	Empowers teams to work independently	Motivates diverse teams to perform	Builds high-performance culture

(continued)

TABLE 4-1 (continued)

DEVELOPING ORGANIZATIONAL CAPABILITIES, PREDICTED BY • ENGAGEMENT • INSIGHT • CURIOSITY	Supports development efforts	Encourages others to develop	Actively supports team members' growth	Systematically builds team's capability	Aids development outside team	Builds organizational capability	Instills culture focused on talent management
CHANGE LEADERSHIP, PREDICTED BY • ENGAGEMENT • DETERMINATION • INSIGHT • CURIOSITY	Accepts change	Supports change	Points out need for change	Makes compelling case for change	Mobilizes others to initiate change	Drives firmwide momentum for change	Embeds culture of change
MARKET UNDERSTANDING, PREDICTED BY • INSIGHT • CURIOSITY	Knows immediate context	Knows general marketplace basics	Investigates market and customer dynamics	Deeply understands market	Generates insights about market's future	Identifies emerging business opportunities	Sees how to transform industry
INCLUSIVENESS, PREDICTED BY • ENGAGEMENT • INSIGHT • CURIOSITY	Accepts different views	Understands diverse views	Integrates other points of view	Functions well across diverse groups	Facilitates engagement between factions	Strategically increases employee diversity	Creates inclusive culture

Source: Egon Zehnder

scores, see the exhibit "Levels of competence.") C-level positions typically require a rating of at least 4 in the competencies critical for those roles, and CEO positions, a rating of at least 5.

You should cascade this process down through the ranks so that you have a clearer idea of the key skills needed to do lower-tier managerial jobs, too. With all positions, however, you must resist the temptation to demand high levels of all competencies, because you'll never find leaders who are perfect. In a study of more than 5,000 executives at 47 companies we conducted with McKinsey, we found that only 1% had an average proficiency score of 6 or better, and just 11% had an average score of 5. So even for the most senior positions, you should seek above-par scores in most competencies and stand-out scores in just two or three.

The next step is to comprehensively assess future leaders' current competencies and their potential for growth. You can do this through a deep review of their work experience; direct questioning; and conversations with their bosses, peers, and direct reports. To get the best information out of people and their colleagues, pose open-ended questions and probe. For instance, to get a read on how much determination managers have, ask about a time something went badly for them and how they responded. To assess their competence at developing organizational capabilities, press for details about the people they've mentored. You should score each person on each hallmark of potential; at Egon Zehnder we use a scale of 1 (emerging) to 4 (extraordinary) for this. You should also score each person on his or her current level of each core competency (using the 1-to-7 scale), creating a snapshot of where he or she stands.

With this information, you can now take the critical third step: predicting where each executive is likely to succeed. Having compared our 30 years' worth of executives' baseline scores with information about their eventual career growth, we can tell you that there are patterns in how individual hallmarks translate to the eventual mastery of leadership competencies. Curiosity is significantly correlated with all eight, so strong scores in it are a prerequisite for anyone being considered for development and promotion. However, the three other hallmarks are each correlated with different competencies and can therefore help us project how leaders will develop. For example, and perhaps not surprisingly, insight is a good predictor of the ability to develop a strategic orientation and market understanding. On a more granular level, we estimate that someone with a score of at least 3 (out of 4) on that hallmark (and on curiosity) should be able to achieve, with the right support, a level 5 competency (out of 7) in strategic orientation. We've also found that people with high determination scores can build the strongest results orientation and change leadership competencies, while those with high engagement scores are likely to be strongest in team leadership, collaboration and influence, and developing organizational capabilities.

Armed with assessments of your emerging leaders' current competencies and potential for growth in each area, you will be in a much better position to make development and succession plans throughout your organization. And that will help you ensure that you have a strong pipeline of people to fill C-suite roles in the future.

The experiences of a major global manufacturer we advised illustrate how this works. The company's CEO was due to retire in a year, and the board was trying to decide who should replace him. When we appraised two internal candidates, X and Y, we found that they had comparable strengths but very different profiles. At the time X, a veteran operator in the company's core business, had a higher level of two competencies critical to the CEO job—results orientation and market understanding. But his lower scores on determination, insight, and curiosity revealed that his potential for growth was more limited. Y, who had come up through the ranks in an emerging business, was by contrast slightly weaker on current competencies but, with strong scores on all the hallmarks, showed significantly more potential to perform well as a CEO. (See the exhibit "Comparing two candidates.")

When the board reviewed these findings, a heated discussion ensued. One senior director argued adamantly for the appointment of X, who had slightly stronger competencies and had deep exposure to the core business. Another director strongly favored Y because of his higher potential. A third director favored an external search given the need for a fully qualified, competitive CEO in just one year.

FIGURE 4-1

Comparing two candidates

When X and Y are evaluated on their current levels of the competencies needed for the CEO position at a global manufacturer, X looks like the better candidate. He is closer to the company's targets for the role.

But when potential is measured, Y begins to shine. His assessment indicates that he could develop his skills beyond X's.

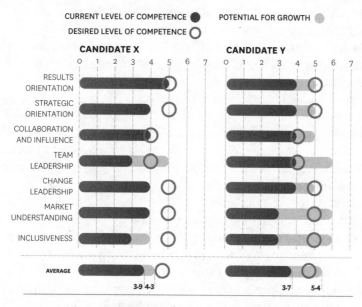

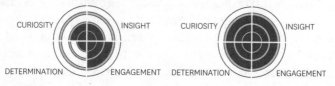

Source: Egon Zehnder

Eventually, the group landed on a creative solution: Ask the current chief executive to stay an extra year, during which he and the board could offer customized development programs to both internal candidates and then monitor their growth.

This is the fourth key step in turning high potentials—at all levels—into leaders: Give them the opportunities, coaching, and support they need to close the gap between their potential and their current competencies. For example, a highly curious, insightful person might be assigned to strategic-planning and innovation projects. Highly determined people should be involved in business-unit turnarounds and cultural-change efforts. Employees with high levels of engagement should be asked to manage small teams and work with key clients.

Well-planned job rotations are also crucial. A survey of 823 highly successful senior executives conducted by Egon Zehnder revealed that the vast majority of them consider stretch assignments and job rotations to be the most important way to accelerate a career. Yet according to a yearly survey of 500 companies by HBS professor Boris Groysberg, these talent practices are actually ones that organizations are the worst at.

The most effective rotations are tailored to individuals' development needs. To strengthen results orientation, for instance, you should move managers through jobs where they'll have P&L responsibility, oversee a start-up initiative, or help implement a restructuring. If the goal is to strengthen someone's inclusiveness competency, rotations through regional businesses and corporatewide functions are a good approach. (For more on how to use assignments to build specific competencies, see the exhibit "Matching the hi-po to the job.")

To help your high potentials build their strengths and make the most of opportunities, you can provide individual coaching and group interventions (which might, say, help their teams create a better sense of identity and purpose). At the global manufacturer that was preparing to replace its CEO, candidate X was given coaching to help him build people-related competencies, while candidate Y was tasked with leading P&L improvements in multiple regions to increase his market understanding and his inclusiveness, which

FIGURE 4-2

Matching the hi-po to the job

Specific kinds of stretch assignments help executives build individual leadership competencies. To strengthen their results orientation, for instance, you can put them in jobs where they'll manage a P&L, run a start-up, or oversee a restructuring.

COMPETENCY	LEADING A LARGE ORGANIZATION	MANAGING A P&L	LEADING MULTIPLE REGIONS OR BUSINESSES	MANAGING A CORPORATE-WIDE FUNCTION	RUNNING A START-UP OPERATION	OVERSEEING A RESTRUCTURING
RESULTS ORIENTATION		●			●	●
STRATEGIC ORIENTATION					●	
COLLABORATION AND INFLUENCE			●	●		
TEAM LEADERSHIP	●	●				●
DEVELOPING ORGANIZATIONAL CAPABILITIES	●			●		
CHANGE LEADERSHIP		●		●	●	●
MARKET UNDERSTANDING			●		●	
INCLUSIVENESS			●	●		

ASSIGNMENT

Source: Egon Zehnder

were significantly below the level the firm thought a "fully qualified" CEO should have. A year later the executives were assessed again, and while both had improved, Y's growth well outpaced that of X, to the point where their competencies were nearly equal. The board decided to offer the CEO job to Y, who went on to successfully implement major change programs and growth initiatives, including mergers and acquisitions. He quadrupled the company's operating income while increasing return on equity from 3% to 11%.

An example of how targeted development works at lower levels comes from an Asia-based global manufacturer, whose CEO was concerned about the slow progress of a diversity initiative. One of its goals was to propel women up the ranks (see the sidebar "Capturing the female advantage"), but none had so far been identified as high potentials by their bosses. The CEO decided to launch a pilot program that involved assessing 10 female managers selected by the head of HR for both potential and competence. The results were striking: The assessments showed that most of them had the attributes necessary to succeed in senior executive roles down the road.

Z, a 30-something corporate planning officer, was one of the women selected. Because of her strong curiosity and engagement, her average potential competency was a high 4.7, but her average current competency score was a low 2.6. And in a couple of areas—strategic orientation and the development of organizational capabilities—she fell well under the target levels for her next possible role and far short of those needed for more-senior jobs.

However, further research showed that the company had failed to help her build those skills. She'd never been asked to manage her own team or lead strategy projects. Her bosses worried about "burdening" someone so "junior" with such big assignments, and Z herself admitted that she lacked confidence.

But the assessment results helped change those attitudes. As the person with the strongest potential scores among all her peers in her department, Z started to get—and embrace—more challenging work. The CEO soon appointed her to head up strategy at a large U.S. subsidiary and supported her by enrolling her in an executive business program and asking the chief human resources officer to serve as

Capturing the Female Advantage

Women are still underrepresented in the top echelons of corporations today. In an effort to learn why, we dug into our global database of ratings of executives' potential and competence, to see how the women compared with their male counterparts. The results were telling:

On average, women's scores trail men's on five of the seven key competencies of leaders. While all the differences are statistically significant, they're large in only two areas: strategic orientation and market understanding.

However, women score higher than men on three of the four hallmarks of potential—curiosity, engagement, and determination—while men have a slightly stronger level of insight. Again, the differences are statistically significant but not too large, except in the case of determination, where the female executives we've assessed scored much higher than their male peers.

How can we reconcile these findings? Why do women have higher potential but less competence than men? We believe it's because women are typically not given the roles and responsibilities they need to hone critical competencies. How can you develop team leadership if you're not given the chance to manage a team, or strengthen your strategic orientation if you never participate in any planning discussions or strategic projects?

her mentor. Z spent a year and a half overseeing multinational projects and proved to be an excellent team builder and strategist. The CEO then asked her to return to headquarters and promoted her to head of alliance management, where she is now effectively leading a sizable group.

The stories of Z and X and Y highlight the fact that for most executive appointments, and especially successions at the top, organizations must make trade-offs between current competence and development potential. A sound estimate of how far each of your top leaders can go will allow you to do that in a less risky, more effective way.

Real Results in Practice

When companies take this approach to leadership development—focusing on potential and figuring out how to help people build the competencies they need for various roles—they see results.

Shortly after Japan Tobacco's privatization, in 1985, the company decided to globalize and to diversify into various businesses, including food and pharmaceuticals. Because of this it needed a new class of leaders. But in Japan hiring executives from the outside has long been highly unusual. In addition, most companies still tend to favor tenure over competence or potential in promotions. Japan Tobacco decided to stick with the first tradition but abandon the second. It began to rigorously assess current leaders' potential and accelerate their development through frequent rotations and focused training. Since then, the company's high potentials have been "owned" by HR and "leased" to key departments under an initiative, currently labeled New Leadership Program, that is constantly tweaked with an eye toward future business scenarios. This approach to leadership development, together with sound strategic decisions, has produced impressive corporate results: After acquiring the British company Gallaher, in 2007, Japan Tobacco became the third-largest global player in the cigarette sector, and thanks to its profitable diversification across geographies and industries, it became the sixth-largest Japanese company in corporate value across all sectors.

Four years ago, Prudential PLC also decided to redesign its leadership development practices to match its global ambitions. At the time, management acknowledged that the existing talent-review process was "assessment-heavy but insight-light" and too focused on current capabilities. Senior leaders set out to revamp it by emphasizing rigorous succession planning across all divisions and regions. Though this change was led by the executive committee and board, development now cascades up rather than down and starts with conversations between HR leaders and line managers, who have been trained to spot future stars. Team managers openly discuss business imperatives, critical roles, and successors, all through the lens of potential, and unit leaders report back up to the group's CHRO and CEO, Tim Rolfe and Mike Wells, sharing details about why people were deemed high potentials and how over time they can grow into different roles across the organization. What have the results been? In 2016, Prudential had 19 openings in its top 100 global roles, including five at the executive committee level, and all but one were filled through internal promotions. The new approach has helped the firm find great leaders even for its most quantitative and analytical businesses, such as asset management, and allowed it to put unexpected people in highly critical roles. For example, Prudential recently announced that it would move Raghu Hariharan, the director of strategy and capital market relations in the group head office, into a position as CFO of the firm's Asia business.

More organizations should follow these models. A scientific approach to talent development—focused on spotting high potentials, understanding their capacity for growth in key competencies, and giving them the experience and support they need to succeed—will be an extraordinary source of competitive advantage in the coming decades. And it will help many more managers transform themselves into the great leaders they were always meant to be.

Originally published in November–December 2017. Reprint R1706E

Making Business Personal

by Robert Kegan, Lisa Lahey, Andy Fleming, and Matthew Miller

TO AN EXTENT THAT we ourselves are only beginning to appreciate, most people at work, even in high-performing organizations, divert considerable energy every day to a second job that no one has hired them to do: preserving their reputations, putting their best selves forward, and hiding their inadequacies from others and themselves. We believe this is the single biggest cause of wasted resources in nearly every company today.

What would happen if people felt no need to do this second job? What if, instead of hiding their weaknesses, they were comfortable acknowledging and learning from them? What if companies made this possible by creating a culture in which people could see their mistakes not as vulnerabilities but as prime opportunities for personal growth?

For three years now, we've been searching for such companies—what we think of as *deliberately developmental organizations*. We asked our extended network of colleagues in academia, consulting, HR, and C-suites if they knew of any organizations that are committed to developing *every one* of their people by weaving personal growth into daily work. We were looking for companies anywhere in the world, public or private, with at least 100 employees and a track record of at least five years.

All that scanning turned up only about 20 companies. In this small pond, two of them stood out: Bridgewater Associates, an East

Coast investment firm, and the Decurion Corporation, a California company that owns and manages real estate, movie theaters, and a senior living center. Both had been meeting our definition of a deliberately developmental organization for more than 10 years. Happily, they were in very different businesses and were willing to be studied in depth.

These companies operate on the foundational assumptions that adults can grow; that not only is attention to the bottom line *and* the personal growth of all employees desirable, but the two are interdependent; that both profitability and individual development rely on structures that are built into every aspect of how the company operates; and that people grow through the proper combination of challenge and support, which includes recognizing and transcending their blind spots, limitations, and internal resistance to change. For this approach to succeed, employees (Decurion prefers to call them members) must be willing to reveal their inadequacies at work— not just their business-as-usual, got-it-all-together selves—and the organization must create a trustworthy and reliable community to make such exposure safe.

As you might guess, that isn't easy or comfortable. But by continually working to meet these linked obligations, deliberately developmental organizations may have found a way to steadily improve performance without simply improving what they're currently doing. That's because progress for their employees means becoming not only more capable and conventionally successful but also more flexible, creative, and resilient in the face of the challenges—for both personal and organizational growth—that these companies deliberately set before them.

The Companies

Bridgewater Associates, based in Westport, Connecticut, manages approximately $150 billion in global investments in two hedge funds— Pure Alpha Strategy and All Weather Strategy—for institutional clients such as foreign governments, central banks, corporate and public pension funds, university endowments, and charitable foundations.

Idea in Brief

The Problem

Most people at work are doing a second job that no one's paying them to do—preserving their reputations, putting their best selves forward, hiding their inadequacies.

The Proposition

What if a company was set up in such a way that instead of hiding their weaknesses, employees used

them as opportunities for both personal and business growth?

The Result

The examples of two very different companies—a hedge fund and a movie theater operator—suggest that it's possible to meld business growth with personal growth in every employee's day-to-day work.

The company began in a two-bedroom apartment in 1975 and is still privately held, currently employing about 1,400 people.

Throughout its nearly four decades, Bridgewater has been recognized as a top-performing money manager; it has won more than 40 industry awards in the past five years alone. At the time of this writing, the Pure Alpha fund had had only one losing year and had gained an average of 14% a year since its founding, in 1991. The All Weather fund, which is designed to make money during good times and bad, has been up 9.5% a year since its launch, in 1996, and delivered an astonishing 34% return from 2009 through 2011, even as the hedge fund industry as a whole underperformed the S&P 500. (The fund apparently did lose money in 2013, according to the *New York Times*.) In both 2010 and 2011 Bridgewater was ranked by *Institutional Investor's Alpha* as the largest and best-performing hedge fund manager in the world. In 2012 the *Economist* credited the firm with having made more money for its investors than any other hedge fund in history. (The previous record holder was George Soros's Quantum Endowment Fund.)

Across the country, in Los Angeles, Decurion employs approximately 1,100 people to manage a portfolio of companies including Robertson Properties Group, with retail and commercial projects in California, Hawaii, and the Pacific Northwest; Pacific Theatres and ArcLight Cinemas; and its newest venture, Hollybrook Senior Living.

In May 2011 *Retail Traffic* magazine recognized Robertson Properties as one of the 100 largest shopping center owners and managers in the United States. Pacific and ArcLight combined have the highest gross per screen in North America. ArcLight's revenues have grown by 72% in four years—from $47 million in 2009 to $81 million in 2013. In 2012 *Forbes* named ArcLight's flagship cinema, ArcLight Hollywood, one of the 10 best movie theaters in the United States.

We have spent more than 100 hours each with Bridgewater and Decurion, observing their practices and interviewing their people, from the most senior leaders to the newest recruits. Virtually no aspect of either company was declared off-limits to us. From the extensive data we collected, we extracted the common traits that, we believe, set these companies apart. We shared our observations and generalizations with both of them and seriously considered their suggestions and impressions. Neither one asked us to alter any of our conclusions.

We acknowledge that a deliberately developmental organization is not for everyone—just as the Jesuits are not the only good choice for every man with a fervent religious calling, or the Navy Seals for every committed commander. But we offer our observations of these two companies as evidence that quests for business excellence and individual fulfillment need not be at odds—and that they can be combined in such a way that each causes the other to flourish.

The Practices

Ordinarily, people acknowledge their vulnerability and imperfections only in rare moments behind closed doors with trusted advisers who swear to protect their privacy. But what we saw at Decurion and Bridgewater was a pervasive effort to enable employees to feel valuable even when they're screwing up—to see limitations not as failures but as their "growing edge," the path to the next level of performance.

Getting to the other side
Transcending your limits—which Bridgewater calls *getting to the other side*—involves overcoming the fight-or-flight response

Leading a Deliberately Developmental Organization

If you are a leader who wants to build a DDO, you should understand that you can't want it just for the company. You must want it for yourself. You must be prepared to participate fully and even to "go first" in making your own limitations public. You must also not want it just to generate extraordinary business results—you must put equal value on leading a company that contributes to the flourishing of its people as an end in itself. You will need patience: It takes time to develop an environment in which people feel safe doing the personal work they'll be asked to do on a regular basis. And you must continually support, defend, and champion this new form of community.

Building an effective DDO also requires that new people be chosen very carefully, with an eye to their appetite for personal reflection and their comfort with examining their own limitations. Even so, it may take 12 to 18 months to be sure that a new hire will do well in this culture, so you should be prepared for a higher rate of turnover than you might otherwise expect. But the people who make it through this induction will most likely display dramatic levels of commitment and engagement.

A sustainable DDO culture depends on a critical mass of people who are together long enough to build strong relationships and gain experience with the practices that facilitate development over time. Thus we question the value of this approach for companies that work on a contractor model and maintain flexibility by depending heavily on free agents, because turnover for them might be too high, and commitment to the organization too low.

---

occasioned by confronting what you are working on about yourself. In a traditional company, root-cause analysis of a problem will stop shy of crossing into an employee's interior world. At Bridgewater, examining a failed investment decision certainly includes a root-cause analysis of the specific data, decision criteria, and steps taken to make the investments. But it goes further, asking, "What is it about how you—the responsible party and shaper of this process— were thinking that might have led to an inadequate decision?"

Consider, for instance, how one Bridgewater employee, John Woody, confronted what CEO Ray Dalio called his "reliability problems," as recorded in a 2013 Harvard Business School case prepared by Jeffrey Polzer and Heidi Gardner. Pulling no punches, Dalio told

Woody that the perception across the organization was that he could not be counted on. Woody's immediate reaction was to angrily reject the feedback. But he did not go off to nurse his grievances or even to uncritically accept what he'd heard. As he began to consider the exchange, he first saw the irony of his reaction. "Here we pride ourselves on being logical and facing the truth, but my initial response was 'You're wrong!' which is me already being illogical," he says. "Even if what he was saying was not true, I was giving him no chance to show me it might be."

After continued reflection and conversations with many people in the organization over many weeks, Woody began to recognize in himself a behavior pattern "that goes all the way back to when I was a kid": He resisted others' control and oversight and was quick to anger when challenged. Looking at the gap between how he wanted to be seen and how he was seen, he realized that he wanted to be "the guy you could give the ball to on the two-yard line"—but that others did not perceive him that way. "People were saying they are unsure I'll even be there to catch it, let alone be able to run it in. And that hurt."

Early on, nearly everyone finds this level of vulnerability disorienting, no matter how enthusiastic he or she may have been about the culture during the hiring process. Dalio acknowledged this fact in a companywide email with the subject line "I fail every day," in which he challenged employees with this question: "Do you worry more about how good you are or about how fast you are learning?" Shifting focus from the former to the latter can lead simultaneously to important personal changes and increased business effectiveness.

When Inna Markus, a member of our research team, asked Woody what progress he was making on his reliability problem, he insisted that he still had a long way to go. Yet it is clear that he has come quite a distance already: "I prioritize more ruthlessly," he says, "pause longer and more thoughtfully before promising things to others, visualize more granularly how I will actually get something done, check in with those who ask things of me more frequently and with more questions, and lean on those around me much more explicitly now than I ever did."

Bridgewater uses a variety of tools and practices to help people learn to treat errors as growth opportunities. For instance, all employees record problems and failures in a companywide "issues log," detailing their own contributions to mistakes. Logging in errors and problems is applauded and rewarded. Not recording a mistake is viewed as a serious breach of duty. Another reflective practice involves a "pain button" app, which is installed on everyone's company-issued iPad and allows employees to share experiences of negative emotions at work—especially those that raise their defenses.

Openly acknowledging those experiences prompts follow-up conversations among the parties involved as they seek to explore the "truth of the situation" and identify ways to address the underlying causes. In one such conversation, a senior manager led members of a work group through a collective diagnosis of why a previous meeting had meandered and failed to reach a productive conclusion. Everyone offered thoughts. The employee who'd led that meeting agreed that he'd gotten wrapped up in defending his own and his colleagues' shoddy work. More than that, he allowed, this was an instance of a bigger, previously unacknowledged tendency he had to worry more about looking good than about achieving the business goal. At most companies a conversation like this would rarely turn toward examining an employee's habitual way of thinking—and if it did, it would be in a closed-door performance review. At Bridgewater such analysis happens in routine meetings with colleagues.

Closing the gaps

Ordinarily, in an effort to protect ourselves, we allow gaps to form— between plans and actions, between ourselves and others, between who we are at work and our "real selves," between what we say at the coffee machine and what we say in the meeting room. These gaps are most often created by the conversations we are *not* having, the synchronicities with others we're *not* achieving, and the work that, out of self-protection, we're avoiding.

To help close these gaps, and to gain more immediate access to the business issues at stake, Bridgewater and Decurion have created discussion formats that allow employees to speak authentically about the personal dimensions of those issues. Bridgewater uses a group probing of an individual's reasoning, as described above. Decurion conducts what it calls a fishbowl conversation, in which several people sit in the middle of a circle of their colleagues. In one such conversation we watched three employees from the IT, marketing, and operations arms of the theater business talk about why a new customer-loyalty program seemed to be stalling. The COO of the theater division suspected that these three key players were not communicating effectively. So she asked them to describe how they were experiencing the situation. The fishbowl format enabled the wider theater managers' group to listen to, learn from, and participate in the conversation. With careful facilitation by another senior manager, the three were able to express the ways in which they each felt shut out or shut down by the other two when decisions were made and information should have been shared. Each also identified some personal trigger or blind spot that had led him or her to shut down one of the others. They could then reach agreement in the presence of colleagues about how to proceed in a different way. Because dialogues like these are routine, people view them as a healthy exercise in sharing vulnerability, rather than a rare and threatening experience.

Over time, exposing one's own vulnerability feels less risky and more worthwhile as people repeatedly witness and participate in conversations about conflict, revelations of their colleagues' weaknesses, and discussions of the undiscussable. In fact, these organizations' most surprising and hopeful accomplishment may be converting their employees' default view of the "unimaginably bad" (*If I risk showing my weaknesses, it will be just horrible!*) into a sense of developmental progress (*If I risk showing my weaknesses, nothing bad will happen to me, I'll probably learn something, and I'll be better for it in the end*). The gap between who they really are and who they think they need to be at work diminishes or even disappears.

Constructive destabilization
Deliberately developmental organizations don't just accept their employees' inadequacies; they cultivate them. Both Bridgewater

Joining a Deliberately Developmental Organization

Ray Dalio and one of us (Bob Kegan) were present for the initial presentation of a Harvard Business School case on Bridgewater. Heidi Gardner, a case coauthor, asked the students toward the end of the discussion, "So how many of you would like to work at Bridgewater?" Just three or four hands went up in a class of 80. "Why not?" she asked. One young woman who'd been an active and impressive contributor to the case conversation replied, "I want people at work to think I'm *better* than I am; I don't want them to see how I *really* am!"

Clearly, people who consider joining a DDO must be willing to show themselves at their worst. And those who join with a distinguished record must be willing to consider big changes in the way they operate. Senior hires at both Decurion and Bridgewater told us: "I heard the words about how it was going to be different, but I didn't understand what that would mean for me."

A DDO makes work deeply engaging; it becomes a way of life. If you want to be able to go home and leave work completely behind, this may not be the right place for you.

The brand of happiness a DDO offers—which arises from becoming a better version of yourself—involves labor pains. Some people might think they would appreciate that but really would not. Others simply cannot imagine that pain at work could lead to something expansive and life changing.

Finally, a DDO is continually evolving. If you expect a workplace to never fall short of its most inspiring principles and guiding ideas, you will quickly be disappointed. A DDO makes space for its people to grow; they must make space for it to develop in return.

and Decurion give a lot of attention to finding a good fit between the person and the role. But here "good fit" means being regularly, though manageably, in over your head—what we call *constructive destabilization*. Constantly finding yourself a bit at sea is destabilizing. Working through that is constructive. At both companies, if it's clear that you can perform all your responsibilities at a high level, you are no longer in the right job. If you want to stay in that job, having finally mastered it, you'll be seen as someone who prefers to coast—and should be working for a different kind of company.

Many organizations offer people stretch assignments. Some commonly rotate high potentials through a series of stretch jobs. At Bridgewater and Decurion all jobs are stretch jobs. As Dalio puts it, "Every job should be like a towrope, so that as you grab hold of the job, the very process of doing the work pulls you up the mountain."

Decurion's ArcLight Cinemas has an elaborate set of practices that allow managers at all levels to facilitate constructive destabilization by matching individuals and groups to appropriate development opportunities. The general manager at each location uses data about individual growth to identify ideal job assignments for every employee every week—assignments meant to serve both the crew member's development and the company's business needs. The management team at each location meets weekly to discuss the goals and performance of each hourly employee and to decide whether someone is ready for more responsibility—say, a reassignment from ticket taker to auditorium scout. (Scouts move from one screen to another looking for ways to assist customers; the job requires a fair amount of initiative, creativity, problem solving, and diplomacy.)

As employees demonstrate new capabilities, their progress is recorded on "competency boards," which are set up in a central back-of-house location in each theater. Colored pins on these boards indicate the capability level of each employee in 15 identified job competencies. This information is used to schedule shift rotations, facilitate peer mentoring, and set expectations for learning as part of a development pipeline. The process meshes individuals' skills with organizational requirements; everyone can see how important individual growth is to the business and how everyone else's job knowledge is expanding. At weekly meetings about a dozen home-office executives and movie house general managers review a dashboard showing theater-level and circuit-level business metrics, which include not only traditional industry data on attendance and sales but also the number of crew members ready for promotion to the first tier of management.

Matching a person to an appropriate stretch job is only half the equation. The other half is aligning the job with the person. Decurion creates numerous opportunities for employees to connect their day-to-day work with what is meaningful to them. At most team meetings, for instance, structured check-ins at the beginning and checkouts at the end allow people to identify ways in which they feel connected to—or disconnected from—the work at hand and their colleagues. A manager might, for instance, describe a communication breakthrough with a colleague and how it has made a shared project even more meaningful. Another manager might report on progress in curbing her tendency to jump in and save the day rather than let the team step up and feel fully accountable.

At one-on-one "touchpoint" meetings with their managers— which happen frequently at all levels of the company—employees can discuss how to realize their personal goals through opportunities tied to Decurion's business needs. One member of a theater crew, for instance, who aspired to become a set decorator (outside Decurion), told us that such a dialogue prompted her general manager to involve her in decor for special events at the cinema—an activity far beyond the scope of her job—in order to align her personal interests with an organizational goal.

For a company to match people with jobs on a continual and granular basis requires that no particular job be dependent on or identified with a single person. That means relinquishing the security of being able to count on someone with long tenure and expertise in a certain role. One senior executive told us, "The purpose of your expertise is to give it away [to the next person coming up]. That sounds wonderful, but in practice—and I have experienced this personally— it is not always easy." Still, all those people constantly growing into ever-changing roles create an organization that becomes more resilient even as it improves the execution of its current strategy.

Everyone is a designer

If something isn't working optimally at Bridgewater or Decurion, it's everyone's responsibility to scrutinize and address the design of the underlying process. For example, frequent "pulse-check huddles" at Decurion allow theater crew members to analyze how a previous set of shows went. In these huddles we saw 17-year-old employees give and receive feedback with their peers and managers about problems in floor operations and ways to improve service for the next set of shows. These young people had learned early on to read the details of the theater's profit-and-loss statement so that they could understand how every aspect of operations (and, by extension, their own actions) contributed to its short- and long-term profitability. When offering ideas for improvements—such as changes in food preparation or readying 3-D glasses for distribution—they spoke in terms of their effect on the guest experience and the financial health of the business.

If a new line of business is being launched, a team will spend lavish amounts of time designing the right process for managing the work. Decurion's employees operate on the assumption that structure drives behavior, so they often focus on subtle aspects of organizational design, such as how offices are arranged, how frequently conversations happen, and what tasks will require collaboration among which people. Unlike Lean Six Sigma and other quality improvement approaches, process improvement at Decurion and Bridgewater integrates a traditional analysis of production errors and anomalies with efforts to correct employees' "interior production errors and anomalies"—that is, their faulty thinking and invalid assumptions.

A major initiative at ArcLight, for example, involved creating teams made up of marketing professionals from the home office and general managers of individual theaters. The company reasoned that if the friction and misunderstanding that typically exist between these groups could be overcome by focusing their collective expertise in small, location-specific teams, improved local film and special-event marketing would produce millions in additional revenue. We observed several such teams holding regular meetings in which they shared ways they were learning to work effectively together and things that still needed improvement. From these discussions it became apparent that audiences varied more from cinema to cinema than the home-office marketers had realized. As they integrated general managers' specialized knowledge about their customers into a nimbler social media strategy, the group's financial performance improved. The managers and marketers stretched themselves to pull together in a new way—and hit new revenue targets. ArcLight's people were as likely to tell us that those revenue targets were designed to stretch people's capabilities as the other way around, illustrating the integrated nature of business and personal development at the company.

Taking the time for growth

When people first hear stories like these, a common reaction is "I can't believe the time they devote to the people processes," usually in a tone suggesting "This is crazy! How can you do this and get anything done?" But Decurion and Bridgewater are not just successful incubators of employee development; they are successful by conventional business benchmarks. Clearly they *do* get things done, and very well.

The simple explanation is that these companies look differently at how they spend time. Conventional organizations may pride themselves on how efficiently they agree on solutions to problems. But do they have so many "efficient" meetings because they haven't identified the personal issues and group dynamics that underlie recurring versions of the same problem? A senior investment analyst at Bridgewater puts it this way: "[The company] calls you on your 'bad,' but, much more than that, it basically takes the position that *you* can do something about this, become a better version of yourself, and when you do, we will be a better company because of it."

The Community

If people must be vulnerable in order to grow, they need a community that will make them feel safe. Deliberately developmental organizations create that community through virtues common to many high-performance organizations—accountability, transparency, and support. But, arguably, they take them to a level that even the most progressive conventional organizations might find uncomfortable.

Accountability

Bridgewater and Decurion are not flat organizations. They have hierarchies. People report to other people. Tough decisions are made.

Businesses are shuttered. People are let go. But rank doesn't give top executives a free pass on the merit of their ideas, nor does it exempt them from the disagreement or friendly advice of those lower down or from the requirement to keep growing and changing to serve the needs of the business and themselves.

Senior leaders are governed by the same structures and practices that apply to other employees. At Decurion they take part in check-ins, sharing their own concerns and failures. At Bridgewater their performance reviews are public, as are all other employees'. And every one of those reviews mentions areas of needed improvement—if they didn't, that would mean those leaders were in the wrong roles.

Thus Dalio explicitly states that he doesn't want his employees to accept a word he says until they have critically examined it for themselves. And Christopher Forman, Decurion's president, has helped create a voluntary 10-week course, The Practice of Self-Management, which many employees have taken several times. The course is taught by Forman and other Decurion leaders, including the head of the real estate company, who told us, "My colleagues didn't feel I'd mastered the material, so they asked me to teach it myself next time around. A typical Decurion move, this caused me to understand the ideas and practices at a much deeper level and to see how to apply them to the businesses."

Transparency

When, in 2008, Decurion's leaders decided to reduce the size of the headquarters staff by 65%, external experts advised them not to tell the employees until the last possible moment, to avoid damaging morale and to prevent the people they wanted to retain from seeking other positions. Instead, they announced their decision immediately.

They enlisted everyone in the transition process, sugarcoated nothing, and shared the financial details behind the decision. Forman explains, "We chose to trust that people could hold this [information]." No resignations followed. Why? "We created a context in which everyone was able to contribute and to grow," Forman says, "both those who wound up staying with the company and those who left." Trusting employees in this way enabled them to reciprocate, to believe that the downsizing was a growth experience that would make them more valuable to the organization—or to future employers.

At Bridgewater every meeting is recorded, and unless proprietary client information was discussed, all employees have access to every recording. All offices are equipped with audio or video recording technology. If an employee's bosses discuss his performance and he wasn't invited to the meeting, the tape is available to him. And he doesn't have to scour every tape to find out if he was the subject of some closed-door conversation. In fact, he's likely to be given a heads-up so that he *will* review the tape.

Initially, Bridgewater's attorneys strenuously advised against this practice. But no longer. In three lawsuits subsequent to its initiation, all three rulings favored Bridgewater precisely because the company could produce the relevant tapes. "And if the tapes show we *did* do something wrong," one senior leader told us, "then we *should* receive a negative judgment."

Support

At both companies everyone from entry-level worker to CEO has a "crew"—an ongoing group that can be counted on to support his or her growth, both professionally and personally. Certainly, good teams in conventional companies also offer moral support. People form bonds, trust one another, and talk about personal things that relate to work and to life beyond work. But these conversations are usually about coping with the potentially destabilizing stresses of the job. In a deliberately developmental organization, the crew is meant to be as much an instrument of that destabilization as a support of one's growth through vulnerability. Decurion and Bridgewater people, including industry leaders whose prior work at other companies had been marked by extraordinary success, mentioned again and again that they felt "ill-equipped," "immobilized," "out on a rope without a net," "beyond my competencies," "repeatedly ineffective with no guarantees I would get it." And yet a team that tried to support someone by reducing destabilization—*restoring* equilibrium—would be seen as doing him no service at all.

Many fine organizations that are not deliberately developmental and may have no interest in becoming so are nonetheless able to create cultures that foster a sense of family fellowship. They demonstrate that a deep sense of human connectedness at work can be unleashed in many ways. But a deliberately developmental organization may create a special kind of community. Experiencing yourself as incomplete or inadequate but still included, accepted, and valued—and recognizing the very capable people around you as also incomplete but likewise valuable—seems to give rise to qualities of compassion and appreciation that can benefit all relationships.

As psychologists, we have sometimes seen this unusual kind of connection among the members of a personal-learning program or a facilitated support group. From such groups we can glimpse the possibility of a new kind of community, as we take up the interior work of our own growth. But these programs are not meant to be permanent or to address the work of the world. By their existence as vibrant, successful companies, Decurion and Bridgewater offer a form of proof that the quest for business excellence and the search for personal realization need not be mutually exclusive—and can, in fact, be essential to each other.

Originally published in April 2014. Reprint R1404B

The Power of Hidden Teams

by Marcus Buckingham and Ashley Goodall

TWO NURSES. SAME JOB; DIFFERENT HOSPITALS. One provides great care for patients, the other doesn't. Why?

Jordan has worked at Stanford Health Care as a clinical nurse in the orthopedic department for the past three years. In a recent interview with us, she described how thrilled she is to be in a role whose entire purpose is helping people get better one by one. In particular, she loves what she calls the interdisciplinary approach, in which the family, the case manager, the physical therapist, the physician, the occupational therapist, the social worker, and the nurse all come together to choose the best care for each patient.

Fritz has been a clinical nurse for about the same amount of time, but he works for a different department in a different hospital. He works the same long hours Jordan does, but unlike her, he is not part of an interdisciplinary unit. He is merely one of 76 nurses, all of them assigned to rotating shifts whose members change from one week to the next, and all of them overseen by two administrators and one nurse supervisor. He is struggling. He embarked on his nursing career with as much passion to help people as Jordan did, but now he's tired, burned out, and thinking about quitting. (Jordan is a real person, whereas Fritz is a composite of several nurses we spoke with.)

Both Jordan and Fritz face incredible daily pressures at work. The job is inherently stressful, the system under strain, the paperwork endless, the emotional burden of caring for the ill weighty, the risk

Idea in Brief

The Problem

Research shows that high levels of employee engagement correlate to more productive and innovative behaviors, better retention, and many other benefits. But if we look across time and geography, we can see that whatever organizations have been doing to engage people isn't working: only about 16 percent of employees are fully engaged, while 84 percent are just going through the motions. The problem is, we don't have a clear understanding of what drives engagement.

The Solution

The most effective way to improve people's health and productivity at work is to focus not on culture or individuals as though they work in isolation but, rather, on their teams. People who do most of their work on a team are twice as likely to be engaged as those who work alone. Organizations that want to increase engagement must first see teams clearly and then direct investments and energies toward improving team experiences.

that errors may lead to lawsuits a constant worry. For Fritz the stress lands heavily. His feeling, as he gets on the bus every morning to head to the hospital, is that he's going through the motions, surviving the experience at work, trying to keep it all at bay. He's just not engaged in his work. Something different is happening for Jordan. Something about her experience at work is lifting her up, not pulling her down. She is fully engaged—and her patients' health outcomes reflect that.

Jordan and Fritz happen to be nurses, but they could be any pair of workers anywhere in the world today, one thriving, the other just muddling through. A question that weighs on employers today is how to make Fritz more like Jordan—how, in other words, to create more highly engaged employees. Organizations' track record at doing this is mixed, to say the least. We wanted to understand what was going wrong.

Why We Care About Engagement, and How We've Been Getting It Wrong

What, exactly, is engagement? At a gut level we know that it has something to do with how involved people are in their work and how enthusiastic they are about it. But by defining engagement more precisely as a set of attitudes, we have been able to measure it—and understand its impact on performance. From research beginning at the Gallup Organization in the 1980s and 1990s, and continued since then by many others (including both of us), we know that certain employee attitudes can help predict productive employee behaviors, and that companies and managers and individuals can take action to improve or change those attitudes. We also know that the attitudes seem to cluster around consistent themes, such as a clear sense of purpose, a commonly held notion of what's valuable or important, feelings of psychological safety, and confidence about the future. We know that when we find these clusters expressed in one person, one team, or one company, we can label that expression "engagement." Finally, we know that engagement—when measured using a few precisely worded statements about the employee's own feelings and experiences—identifies a situation at work that leads to productivity, innovation, retention, and much more.

But when we look at aggregated levels of engagement across time and across countries, it quickly becomes clear that whatever organizations have been doing to improve these outcomes—from efforts

FIGURE 6-1

The sad state of employee engagement

The vast majority of employees globally aren't fully engaged with their work.

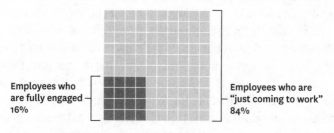

Employees who
are fully engaged
16%

Employees who are
"just coming to work"
84%

Source: ADP Research Institute, 2019

around company culture to rigorous performance management—isn't working. One of us (Marcus), building on his engagement work with the Gallup Organization, recently joined the ADP Research Institute (ADPRI) to lead its investigations into people and performance at work. He and his team have now completed the most extensive and methodologically consistent global study of engagement yet undertaken, in which a representative sample of working adults from 19 countries—1,000 respondents in each country—were asked to respond to eight statements designed to measure engagement reliably. (Read more about the study in the sidebar "The ingredients of engagement.") This study reveals, among many other findings, that only about 16% of employees are fully engaged at work, like Jordan, while about 84% are just going through the motions, like Fritz.

These results are no happier than those revealed in earlier surveys conducted over the years by Gallup and others. And since we know that employee engagement drives employee productivity at the level of the business unit, it's hardly surprising that over the past 40 years the growth in per-person productivity in the United States has also been anemic, hovering barely above 1% a year, while other developed countries, such as the UK and Germany, seem to be doing even worse. Clearly we need to find another way.

The key is to understand what *actually* drives engagement. For years we've been getting this wrong. Most of us, when evaluating the difference between Jordan's and Fritz's experiences, tend to jump to one of two explanations. The first is that something about Jordan's hospital works for her, and something about Fritz's hospital doesn't work for him. So to improve his life and performance at work, the focus should be Fritz's hospital as a whole: It should offer more support to its nurses. Its commitment to work/life balance should be more explicit. It should talk up its "talent brand" and describe ever more clearly the sort of nurses it seeks to attract and how it wants them to behave so that all can better understand how they ought to perform. The common name for this idea is *culture*—and although companies that prioritize culture, and thereby the experience of their people, are taking an important first step, addressing the employee experience at the company level is an incomplete solution.

The second explanation goes to the other end of the spectrum. Rather than focusing on the broad notion of culture, it explains the differences in performance and engagement between Jordan and Fritz in terms of who they are as individuals: Something's right about Jordan, and something's less than right about Fritz. The prescription then becomes to help Fritz become more engaged by giving him feedback on how he's doing, developing him with more training, moving him around in hopes that a different role will bring different results, or, ultimately, replacing him with a nurse who will, with luck, be more like Jordan.

In essence, we have treated organizations like increasingly complex machines in which the humans are but component parts and in which the solutions to any ills involve tweaking the system from the top—by addressing culture broadly—or by upgrading the individual components, the humans, themselves.

But the ADPRI study that undergirds this article reveals a disarmingly simple, and hitherto largely neglected, way of increasing someone's health and productivity at work. It turns out that the most effective way to improve Fritz's lot, and that of his patients and his hospital, is to focus not on culture or on individuals as though they work in isolation but, rather, on what makes Jordan's experience shine: her team.

The Case for Teams

To find the most-effective levers for creating engagement, we set about analyzing a number of variables for their power to explain why a particular employee might be fully engaged. Were older workers more disillusioned, and thus less likely than younger people to be fully engaged? Was high engagement best explained by a higher level of education? Did work status make a difference—meaning part-time workers were more engaged than full-time workers, or vice versa? The ADPRI study probed all these variables and more in an effort to discover which of them could best explain engagement and productivity. And as it turned out, the most powerful factor was simply whether or not respondents reported doing most of their

FIGURE 6-2

The power of teams

The share of employees who are fully engaged more than doubles if they are on teams.

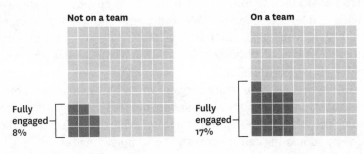

Not on a team

On a team

Fully
engaged —
8%

Fully
engaged —
17%

Source: ADP Research Institute, 2019

work on a team. Those who did were more than *twice as likely* to be fully engaged as those who said they did most of their work alone. The local, ground-level experience of work—the people they worked with and their interactions with them—trumped everything else.

That makes sense. According to the ADPRI study, most work—in every industry, in every region of the world, and at every level in an organization—is actually teamwork; 83% of workers say they do most of their work in teams (although, as we'll see, some teams are far more engaging than others). The team is the reality of your experience at work. You have responsibilities that seem to be connected to other people's responsibilities; you have strengths that seem to be complemented by those of others; you have people over your left shoulder and your right, looking out for you, keeping your confidences, offering their reactions to your work, sharing your idea of what "good" is, chipping in when you seem overwhelmed, and giving their input when you get stuck. The quality of this team experience is the quality of your work experience.

To feel like you're a part of a team doesn't require you to be oriented to the company culture; neither does it require a particular training course or development initiative. Instead, it depends on whether your team leader and your teammates show up every day, talk to you, lean in to you, and support you. Your experience of your team drives many things: how productive you are at work; how happy you are at work; how creative, innovative, and resilient you are; and how long you choose to stay with your company. In other words, when it comes to your work, great teams and teamwork aren't a nice-to-have; they're a must-have.

The best—indeed, according to our research, the only—way to help Fritz feel and perform more like Jordan is to start with the needs of his team. And if we want to increase engagement and productivity at work, we must first understand why it's difficult for organizations to *see* teams at work and how that's now changing. Then we must direct our investments and energies at improving those team experiences.

Seeing Teams

Organizations can see boxes and lines on the org chart, but those fail to account for many actual teams. When the same ADPRI study asked respondents if they worked on more than one team—and how many of those teams could be found on the org chart—64% said yes, and of those, three-quarters said their additional teams didn't show up in the directory. Most work is teamwork, but about half the teams where it happens are invisible to companies.

That blindness stems from our tools. "We shape our tools, and then our tools shape us," the saying goes. The tools that help us "see" our people—so-called human capital management tools that ensure that people are paid properly, are accounted for by the right departments, and are billed against the correct budgets—are all extensions of enterprise resource planning (ERP) tools, a significant part of whose function is organizing people into the right buckets. The source of truth regarding who lives in which bucket—marketing, say, or finance—and in which box in that bucket, is the human resources department. If a manager wants to formally add someone to his or her team, that manager has to call up HR and ask permission to move

The Ingredients of Engagement

The ADP Research Institute 2019 study set out to measure the levels of engagement of more than 19,000 workers across the globe and to identify the factors most likely to attract and keep them. The study focused on aspects of engagement that an organization can influence rather than those that are usually beyond its control—such as political, economic, or individual concerns.

ADP sought to capture the essence of engagement by asking every team member about the extent to which he or she agreed with eight simple statements, on a 5-point scale from "strongly disagree" to "strongly agree." These statements, the early formulations of which were first presented by researchers at Gallup and which have since been refined by researchers at Deloitte, Cisco, ADP, and several other companies, have proved to be the most reliable and powerful way we have discovered to date to explain the difference between the best work experiences and the rest.

The eight statements (taken verbatim from the ADPRI study) capture the emotional and attitudinal precursors to engagement and the productive employee behaviors that flow as a result.

1. I am really enthusiastic about the mission of my company.
2. At work, I clearly understand what is expected of me.
3. In my team, I am surrounded by people who share my values.
4. I have the chance to use my strengths every day at work.
5. My teammates have my back.
6. I know I will be recognized for excellent work.
7. I have great confidence in my company's future.
8. In my work, I am always challenged to grow.

---

a "head count" (which basically means a paycheck) from one box to another. Approvals have to be applied for, budgets have to be consulted, permissions must be granted up and down the chain, until finally white smoke appears from the chimney and lo and behold, the new head count appears in a new box on the org chart.

What this hides, of course, is how work actually gets done. In the real world, team leaders are pulling team members onto new teams all the time. Some of those teams last three weeks, some three months—which is why the ADPRI study asked about differences

Importantly, respondents are not directly rating their managers or their companies on anything—they are rating only their own feelings and experiences. That's because people are horribly unreliable raters of other people. When we ask someone to rate another person, or a company, on an abstract quality such as empathy or vision or strategic thinking or inclusiveness, the response tells us more about the person doing the rating than about the person or company being rated. To get good data we must ask people only about their own experiences.

The study included 19 countries and used exactly the same methodology in each one—1,000 participants per country, stratified to match the workforce demographic. Every participant was presented with the same eight statements, and to ensure apples-to-apples comparisons, a correction was applied in the data analysis to take into account our finding that different nationalities have meaningfully different response patterns to rating scales. (Brazilians, for example, tend to skew toward the positive, and Japanese toward the negative, while Brits inevitably sit somewhere in the middle.)

By analyzing response patterns, we were able to place each person in one of two categories. We use the term *fully engaged* to describe people who answered virtually all the statements very positively. It turns out that they are also far more likely to be viewed by their managers as highly productive and far less likely to quit the organization in the following six months. And we use the term *coming to work* to describe those who respond neutrally or negatively to most of these statements. People in this category are not necessarily destructive or harmful to their organizations, but neither are they passionately committed. They are merely selling their time and talent to get by in the world. Clearly, Jordan is in the first of these categories, and Fritz is in the second.

between ground-level reality and org-chart theory. It found that the source of truth about what teams exist and who is on them is actually the team leader, not HR. Further, a team leader isn't a name in a box but, rather, *anyone* who has successfully recruited a group of people to work on something.

In other words, teams are not defined by who reports to whom in which department on an org chart. They *emerge* from a multitude of requests and acceptances, none of which HR sees, some of which are overlapping, many of which are ephemeral, and all of which are where people's actual experience of work truly resides. Our current tools are blind to this reality, and so, therefore, are we. We can't see our teams, so we can't see our work.

All this is changing, however. Our always-on mobile phones and the app-ification they have engendered mean that developers are now building tools that busy team leaders and members voluntarily use. These are not the traditional goal-setting, performance-rating, form-filling tools—the kind that HR has to coerce people into engaging with. Instead they are tools such as Slack, Jira, and Cisco's Webex Teams, which meet team leaders and members in stride and help them get real work done through people. Although these are productivity tools, focused primarily on work rather than team building, organizations are starting to use their "exhaust" data to see who is reaching out to whom, who is inviting whom to join a project, who is relying on whom to meet a deadline. In other words, we are starting to actually see the dynamic, ephemeral, informal, contingent, and fluid teams of the real world of work. So now, finally, we can investigate what real teams—and in particular, the very best teams—look like in the wild.

Understanding how teams operate would mean an end to many of the initiatives that organizations currently rely on to address engagement and performance. For example, we wouldn't do a once-a-year engagement survey of the whole organization, break down the results according to the departments and divisions on the org chart, and pretend that we'd found anything useful. Instead we would simply analyze the data coming out of teams, in real time. We wouldn't design so much work around *extrinsic* incentives (pay, promotion, titles, and so forth), as though *intrinsic* incentives (meaning, growth, relationships, and so forth) were impossible to measure; we would instead measure those things team by team, where they make the most difference. The organization's goals wouldn't cascade down to individuals through the who-reports-to-whom lines on the org chart, because those lines don't encompass anywhere near all the real teams in the company. And performance reviews wouldn't follow those same lines, because most performance occurs outside the boxes. Instead, critical initiatives—around innovation, around diversity—and performance measurement would be deployed through the actual teams where work is being done.

On the team level, people wouldn't be invited to be team leaders simply because they were good at being team members; we can see and measure teams' performance, so we know what experiences the best leaders create. We would make informed decisions about how many people should be on a given team, because we would know how team performance is affected by the span of a team leader's control—the number of people the leader is responsible for. We would train specific teams together, according to their needs and to build their unique strengths, rather than chasing some generic "teamwork" skill.

In other words, by finally being able to see dynamic, ephemeral, local teams, we would better fight the real war for talent: not just attracting the best people, but getting from them the best that they, uniquely, have to offer.

The Best Teams

Though feeling like you're on a team is fundamental to engagement, it's true that some teams are far more engaging than others. In the most engaged teams—the top quartile—59% of members are fully engaged, whereas in the bottom quartile 0% are. The ADPRI study strongly suggests that a number of key factors separate the best teams from the rest. From those we can draw the following conclusions for leaders about how to improve their teams:

Focus on trust
Our data immediately pinpoints the biggest differentiator between high- and low-performing teams: trust in the team leader. Team members who *strongly agree* that they trust their team leader are *eight times* as likely to be fully engaged as those who don't. This trust must be deep and without question. A team member who merely *agrees* that she trusts her team leader shows roughly the same level of engagement as does someone who actively distrusts his team leader. For trust to matter, it must be extreme.

FIGURE 6-3

The power of trust

As noted, the share of employees who are fully engaged more than doubles if they are on a team. It more than doubles again if they strongly trust the team leader.

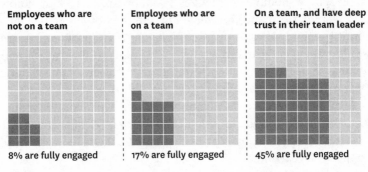

Employees who are not on a team	Employees who are on a team	On a team, and have deep trust in their team leader
8% are fully engaged	17% are fully engaged	45% are fully engaged

Source: ADP Research Institute, 2019

We can go further, to identify the core components of that trust. That is, we know what activities a team leader must engage in to build extreme trust with her team members. In analyzing the ADPRI study to ascertain which concepts are most associated with trust, we discovered that strong agreement with two statements from our survey, "At work, I clearly understand what is expected of me" and "I have the chance to use my strengths every day at work," corresponds with a high level of trust in the team leader. This suggests that despite the fluidity of today's working world, the best team leaders can help each team member feel both understood and focused. *Know me for my best, and then focus my work around that:* These are the fundamental needs of every team member, and the foundation of any high-performing team.

As part of the qualitative analysis that accompanies any quantitative research, we interviewed a woman we'll call Kyona, a social media manager in a professional services firm, because the data revealed that she and her fellow team members were highly engaged. She described one small way in which a busy team leader can stop the flow of work to show a team member that her strengths are noticed and translated into ongoing expectations. "There was this one team meeting where everyone was spinning around and around, and I jumped in, simplified the issue, and solved it," she said. "My team leader paid attention to that. She called me the Calm in the Chaos, the pragmatic one who avoids getting wrapped up in debate. She named it, pointed it out to the rest of the team, and now in meetings, whenever we get stuck, everyone just naturally turns to me." Kyona and her team leader have taken this understanding beyond team meetings and into their weekly check-ins, during which Kyona shares her priorities and she and her team leader chat about course corrections and small shifts of focus. Over time each check-in serves as both a nudge toward the right outcomes and a reminder that Kyona's strengths are top-of-mind for her team leader. The high level of engagement that the members of Kyona's team feel comes in large part from the trust her team leader builds in this way.

Design teams for human attention

The importance of trust leads us in turn to what we consider to be the most important insight from the ADPRI study about how to create engaged teams. Its outlines appear when we look more closely at our two nurses at work.

In Fritz's department, 76 nurses report to one nurse manager. No matter how brilliant that manager is, she simply cannot address the needs and priorities of every nurse every week—with the result that Fritz and his colleagues feel unseen, unheard, and alone as they face their daily challenges.

In contrast, Jordan's department actually has more nurses and nurse assistants—97—but that's just how things look on the org chart. Stanford Health Care is pioneering ways to make frequent, light-touch attention between team member and team leader the fundamental design principle of work. According to its CHRO, David Jones, the organization has not only deliberately put patients at the center of the dynamic teams that spring up every day (this is the "interdisciplinary approach" that so engages Jordan) but is also deploying an ADP team creation, engagement measurement, and check-in tool called StandOut to every employee. It enables team members to get the attention they need from their team leaders, whether their team is visible on the org chart or just popped up yesterday to focus on a particular patient.

The data from Stanford Health Care—together with other research from Cisco, Deloitte, ADP, Mission Health, and Levi's—tells us that frequent attention to the work of each team member is what we might call the *anchor ritual* of team leadership. These organizations have all instituted a simple weekly conversation between team leaders and each of their team members and have been able to measure increases in engagement as a function of the frequency of these check-ins.

The check-ins address two simple questions—What are your priorities this week, and How can I help?—and serve to ensure that each team member receives the attention needed to do his or her best work. They are focused on the future and on what energizes each team member; they are strengths-based, not remedial.

The data makes an unambiguous case that the frequency of conversations is critical. An earlier ADPRI study at Stanford Health Care showed that team leaders who check in once a week see, on average, engagement levels 21 points higher than what those who check in only once a month see. A recent Cisco study yielded comparable data. And according to Jones, "We can see from our data that teams with more-frequent check-ins have dramatically higher levels of engagement; so, moving forward, we are going to keep experimenting with smaller, more patient-centered, more agile teams, and keep investigating the link between span of control and patient outcomes—and all because we can see the link between attention, teams, and patient care."

The most-engaged teams—and the most-effective team leaders—understand that the currency of engagement is real, human attention. This helps us answer a long-standing question about the optimal span of control in all organizations. Some research puts the number at eight to 10, whereas some workplaces, such as call centers, push the limits with spans as great as 70 team members to one supervisor. Pinpointing the check-in, and the frequent attention it provides, as the key driver of engagement shows that "span of control" is more accurately *span of attention*. The research reveals that for people to be engaged, the span of control must allow each team leader to check in, one on one, with each team member every week of the year. Any relayering, delayering, or org redesign that prevents such frequent attention will ultimately lead to disengagement, burnout, and turnover.

Learn together

How can we help teams improve? One problem is that to teach employees to be better team members, organizations typically send them to a class on, say, empathy, active listening, or project management—alone. They are taught these skills in a context completely separate from the teams where they will actually employ them. Then, when there still seems to be something wrong with how teammates interact, comes a second problematic intervention: They are sent to workshops and offsites featuring trust falls and other team-building activities that are unrelated to the actual teamwork— and so teach nothing about trusting one another in the context of work and nothing about making that work more transparent and predictable.

There's a different way. At Cisco, where one of us (Ashley) is a senior vice president, rather than teaching "teamwork skills" to employees and team leaders in isolation, the training is brought to the team through the Power of Teams program. Each session of the program begins with a discussion of engagement on *this* team, *right now*. Team members get to know their current teammates through the lens of their strengths. From those ingredients, the team builds new habits and rituals to accelerate its members' growth together through their work together, on this particular team at this particular moment in time. Cisco has applied this specific, real-time, one-size-fits-one-team approach to team improvement more than 600 times in the past three years. The company has learned that helping each team to understand how it's doing and to find new approaches rooted in the people on the team and the work in front of them is far more valuable than teaching abstract teaming skills to one person at a time. Such has been the impact of the program at Cisco that leaders have requested more than 400 sessions for the next 12 months alone.

Put team experience above team location

Two recent labor trends have provoked much chatter in big companies thinking about engagement: remote work and gig work. The sense seems to be that remote work detracts from engagement and that gig work is a lonely, atomized experience. The past few years have seen a persistent pull to get workers back into the office. From Yahoo CEO Marissa Mayer's 2013 edict that all workers must come to the office every day to more-recent rollbacks of work-from-home policies at Aetna and IBM along with our current fixation on open-plan workspaces and the location of the next new corporate head-quarters—the prevailing wisdom appears to be that remote work is neither as productive nor as engaging as colocated work; that if we want people to collaborate and innovate with one another effectively on teams, they need to be bumping into one another in hallways and chatting with one another at coffee stations.

The ADPRI study has shown us something surprisingly different: First off, 23% of workers report that they work from home most of the time, and they turn out to be more engaged than colocated workers—20% versus 15.8%. Furthermore, better than half of those remote workers (55%), far from feeling isolated, report that they feel part of a team. And of those who feel like part of a team, 27% are fully engaged at work. By contrast, only 17% of colocated team members who report they feel part of a team are fully engaged.

Having combined these initial findings and looked at them through the lens of team versus non team rather than remote versus colocated, we can say for sure that to engage your people, you should avoid mandating that they show up at the office every day, and also that all the time you spend helping your remote workers join, get to know the other members of, and feel supported by their teams will pay off in the form of more-engaged workers. Engagement is about *whom* you work with, not *where*.

Make all work more like gig work

With the rise of the gig economy have come concerns that gig workers are socially isolated. But the ADPRI study revealed that gig work is more engaging than traditional work—18% of gig-only workers (meaning both full- and part-time contract or contingent workers) are fully engaged, versus 15% of traditional workers (those not participating in the gig economy). That's because of the top two reasons people reported loving their gig work: It gives them far more control over their working lives, and they feel more freedom to do work they love (both of which help explain why the ADPRI study shows that the most common title gig workers bestow on themselves is "president").

Consistent with this, when respondents were asked to describe their work status in detail—one full-time job, two part-time jobs for two companies, one full-time job and one part-time job with the same company, and so on—it turned out that by far the most engaging work status (25% fully engaged) was this: one full-time job and one part-time job for a different company. The full-time job brings stability and benefits, while the part-time role—like gig work—brings flexibility and the chance for the person to do something he or she truly enjoys (along with additional income).

These findings reveal not only that gig work can be very engaging but that it actually contains elements that can and should be transplanted into our traditional work. We should try to make all work more like gig work: Employees should have more control over their work and a greater chance to do work they love. They should have the best of both worlds: one predictable, stable role with a "home team" (more often than not, the static team depicted on the org chart) and one "side hustle"—a series of opportunities to join dynamic teams inside the same organization. Their greatest value to any of these teams may well be the particular, wonderful, and weird set of strengths they possess. This is not the usual way of designing either work or career paths, but it may be the most engaging.

The Weirdness Orchestrators

What all this evidence tells us is that for the Fritzes of the world—which is to say all of us, from time to time and place to place—a focus on the ends of the seesaw, on reinforcing company culture on the one hand or trying to zero in on each individual in isolation on the other, won't deliver what companies want or, more important, what people at work need.

Organizations should pay less attention to the ends of the continuum and instead focus on the fulcrum of work: the team. When confronted with a performance problem or an innovation opportunity or anything else, we should ask, "How can we address this through our teams?"

First, the information architecture must be in place—we need to see the teams. We need to find and use technologies that will allow team leaders to tell those leading their organizations, in real time, who is on each team they lead. These technologies must be helpful to team leaders so that they will use them *voluntarily* to understand and better support their team members in the rhythms of daily work, because only from voluntary and ongoing use will we see in real time who is working with whom.

Second, we have to be more specific in how we think about leadership. Leadership roles within a large organization are many and varied, of course, but the weight of the evidence is that the most important of these, and thus the one that must be our highest priority, is the role of team leader. Of all the factors that create the experiences that distinguish the best teams, the most important is the actions of the team leader, and how he or she builds trust and gives attention. Thus we should select, train, reward, and promote leaders not on the basis of an abstract list of generic leadership competencies but, rather, on their appetite for team leadership and their demonstrable track record as team leaders.

Third, we need to break the shackles of the org chart. The fundamental lesson of the research is that work happens on teams, whether they are overlapping, dynamic, spontaneous or designed, long-lived or short-lived. The real world of work is messy. We must push into the richness of real teams doing real work, and we must ask new questions: Do large successful teams have the same habits and rhythms as small successful teams? In how many ways do teams start? Do the best ways for team members to share information vary according to the type of team they're on? Are some ways demonstrably better than others, in terms of their impact on team engagement? Do virtual teams adopt a cadence different from that of colocated teams?

Beyond that, should we reimagine our organizations as places where everyone has a home team plus one or more gig teams? Should we then push further, and consider careers not as a series of steps up the org ladder but as an accumulation of experiences across many dynamic teams? Can we use our teams, with their inherent flexibility, to rethink how we structure the "people stuff" in our companies—compensation, promotion, development, and succession? And if so, do we need the org chart at all?

For team leaders, the emphasis needs to shift from the generic to the specific. We need to be clear that the job of a team leader is simply, and challengingly, this: to create, day in and day out, an experience on the team that allows each person to offer his or her unique best, and then to meld those contributions into something no individual could do alone. We need to anchor this job in rituals and measures, all designed to help magnify what the best teams do: the weekly check-in; frequent discussion with each person and with the team as a whole about where people can employ their strengths; and use of the eight items in our methodology to gauge progress, not for the purpose of accountability but, rather, for illumination and course correction.

And here, finally, we see the core purpose of teams: They are the best method we humans have ever devised to make each person's uniqueness useful. We know that the frequent use of strengths leads to high performance, and we know that strengths vary from person to person. High-functioning teams are essential to a high-functioning organization because they create more opportunities for each person to use his or her strengths by enabling the tasks at hand to be divided according to the strengths on offer. Teams make weirdness useful. They are a mechanism for integrating the needs of the individual and the needs of the organization. If we can get them right, we solve a lot of problems. Ultimately, then, to help our people become fully engaged, we need to help our team leaders see that they are our weirdness orchestrators, our quirk capturers—that theirs is the most important job in our companies, and that only they can do it.

Originally published in May 2019. Reprint H04XJ8

The Performance Management Revolution

by Peter Cappelli and Anna Tavis

WHEN BRIAN JENSEN TOLD HIS AUDIENCE of HR executives that Colorcon wasn't bothering with annual reviews anymore, they were appalled. This was in 2002, during his tenure as the drugmaker's head of global human resources. In his presentation at the Wharton School, Jensen explained that Colorcon had found a more effective way of reinforcing desired behaviors and managing performance: Supervisors were giving people instant feedback, tying it to individuals' own goals, and handing out small weekly bonuses to employees they saw doing good things.

Back then the idea of abandoning the traditional appraisal process—and all that followed from it—seemed heretical. But now, by some estimates, more than one-third of U.S. companies are doing just that. From Silicon Valley to New York, and in offices across the world, firms are replacing annual reviews with frequent, informal check-ins between managers and employees.

As you might expect, technology companies such as Adobe, Juniper Systems, Dell, Microsoft, and IBM have led the way. Yet they've been joined by a number of professional services firms (Deloitte, Accenture, PwC), early adopters in other industries (Gap, Lear, OppenheimerFunds), and even General Electric, the longtime role model for traditional appraisals.

Without question, rethinking performance management is at the top of many executive teams' agendas, but what drove the change in this direction? Many factors. In a recent article for *People + Strategy,* a Deloitte manager referred to the review process as "an investment of 1.8 million hours across the firm that didn't fit our business needs anymore." One *Washington Post* business writer called it a "rite of corporate kabuki" that restricts creativity, generates mountains of paperwork, and serves no real purpose. Others have described annual reviews as a last-century practice and blamed them for a lack of collaboration and innovation. Employers are also finally acknowledging that both supervisors and subordinates despise the appraisal process—a perennial problem that feels more urgent now that the labor market is picking up and concerns about retention have returned.

But the biggest limitation of annual reviews—and, we have observed, the main reason more and more companies are dropping them—is this: With their heavy emphasis on financial rewards and punishments and their end-of-year structure, they hold people accountable for past behavior at the expense of improving current performance and grooming talent for the future, both of which are critical for organizations' long-term survival. In contrast, regular conversations about performance and development change the focus to building the workforce your organization needs to be competitive both today and years from now. Business researcher Josh Bersin estimates that about 70% of multinational companies are moving toward this model, even if they haven't arrived quite yet.

The tension between the traditional and newer approaches stems from a long-running dispute about managing people: Do you "get what you get" when you hire your employees? Should you focus mainly on motivating the strong ones with money and getting rid of the weak ones? Or are employees malleable? Can you change the way they perform through effective coaching and management and intrinsic rewards such as personal growth and a sense of progress on the job?

With traditional appraisals, the pendulum had swung too far toward the former, more transactional view of performance, which became hard to support in an era of low inflation and tiny merit-pay budgets. Those who still hold that view are railing against the recent

Idea in Brief

The Problem

By emphasizing individual accountability for past results, traditional appraisals give short shrift to improving current performance and developing talent for the future. That can hinder long-term competitiveness.

The Solution

To better support employee development, many organizations are dropping or radically changing their annual review systems in favor of giving people less formal, more frequent feedback that follows the natural cycle of work.

The Outlook

This shift isn't just a fad—real business needs are driving it. Support at the top is critical, though. Some firms that have struggled to go entirely without ratings are trying a "third way": assigning multiple ratings several times a year to encourage employees' growth.

emphasis on improvement and growth over accountability. But the new perspective is unlikely to be a flash in the pan because, as we will discuss, it is being driven by business needs, not imposed by HR.

First, though, let's consider how we got to this point—and how companies are faring with new approaches.

How We Got Here

Historical and economic context has played a large role in the evolution of performance management over the decades. When human capital was plentiful, the focus was on which people to let go, which to keep, and which to reward—and for those purposes, traditional appraisals (with their emphasis on individual accountability) worked pretty well. But when talent was in shorter supply, as it is now, developing people became a greater concern—and organizations had to find new ways of meeting that need.

From accountability to development

Appraisals can be traced back to the U.S. military's "merit rating" system, created during World War I to identify poor performers for discharge or transfer. After World War II, about 60% of U.S. companies were using them (by the 1960s, it was closer to 90%). Though seniority rules determined pay increases and promotions for unionized workers, strong merit scores meant good advancement prospects for managers. At least initially, *improving* performance was an afterthought.

And then a severe shortage of managerial talent caused a shift in organizational priorities: Companies began using appraisals to develop employees into supervisors, and especially managers into executives. In a famous 1957 HBR article, social psychologist Douglas McGregor argued that subordinates should, with feedback from the boss, help set their performance goals and assess themselves—a process that would build on their strengths and potential. This "Theory Y" approach to management—he coined the term later on—assumed that employees wanted to perform well and would do so if supported properly. ("Theory X" assumed you had to motivate people with material rewards and punishments.) McGregor noted one drawback to the approach he advocated: Doing it right would take managers several days per subordinate each year.

By the early 1960s, organizations had become so focused on developing future talent that many observers thought that tracking past performance had fallen by the wayside. Part of the problem was that supervisors were reluctant to distinguish good performers from bad. One study, for example, found that 98% of federal government employees received "satisfactory" ratings, while only 2% got either of the other two outcomes: "unsatisfactory" or "outstanding." After running a well-publicized experiment in 1964, General Electric concluded it was best to split the appraisal process into separate discussions about accountability and development, given the conflicts between them. Other companies followed suit.

Back to accountability

In the 1970s, however, a shift began. Inflation rates shot up, and merit-based pay took center stage in the appraisal process. During that period, annual wage increases really mattered. Supervisors often had discretion to give raises of 20% or more to strong performers, to distinguish them from the sea of employees receiving basic cost-of-living raises, and getting no increase represented a substantial pay cut. With the stakes so high—and with antidiscrimination laws so recently on the books—the pressure was on to award pay more objectively. As a result, accountability became a higher priority than development for many organizations.

Three other changes in the zeitgeist reinforced that shift:

First, Jack Welch became CEO of General Electric in 1981. To deal with the long-standing concern that supervisors failed to label real differences in performance, Welch championed the forced-ranking system—another military creation. Though the U.S. Army had devised it, just before entering World War II, to quickly identify a large number of officer candidates for the country's imminent military expansion, GE used it to shed people at the bottom. Equating performance with individuals' inherent capabilities (and largely ignoring their potential to grow), Welch divided his workforce into "A" players, who must be rewarded; "B" players, who should be accommodated; and "C" players, who should be dismissed. In that system, development was reserved for the "A" players—the high-potentials chosen to advance into senior positions.

Second, 1993 legislation limited the tax deductibility of executive salaries to $1 million but exempted performance-based pay. That led to a rise in outcome-based bonuses for corporate leaders—a change that trickled down to frontline managers and even hourly employees—and organizations relied even more on the appraisal process to assess merit.

Third, McKinsey's War for Talent research project in the late 1990s suggested that some employees were fundamentally more talented than others (you knew them when you saw them, the thinking went). Because such individuals were, by definition, in short supply, organizations felt they needed to take great care in tracking and rewarding them. Nothing in the McKinsey studies showed that fixed personality traits actually made certain people perform better, but that was the assumption.

So, by the early 2000s, organizations were using performance appraisals mainly to hold employees accountable and to allocate rewards. By some estimates, as many as one-third of U.S. corporations—and 60% of the *Fortune* 500—had adopted a forced-ranking system. At the same time, other changes in corporate life made it harder for the appraisal process to advance the time-consuming goals of improving individual performance and developing skills for future roles. Organizations got much flatter, which dramatically increased the number of subordinates that supervisors had to manage. The new norm was 15 to 25 direct reports (up from six before the 1960s). While overseeing more employees, supervisors were also expected to be individual contributors. So taking days to manage the performance issues of each employee, as Douglas McGregor had advocated, was impossible. Meanwhile, greater interest in lateral hiring reduced the need for internal development. Up to two-thirds of corporate jobs were filled from outside, compared with about 10% a generation earlier.

Back to development . . . again

Another major turning point came in 2005: A few years after Jack Welch left GE, the company quietly backed away from forced ranking because it fostered internal competition and undermined collaboration. Welch still defends the practice, but what he really supports is the general principle of letting people know how they are doing: "As a manager, you owe candor to your people," he wrote in the *Wall Street Journal* in 2013. "They must not be guessing about what the organization thinks of them." It's hard to argue against candor, of course. But more and more firms began questioning how useful it was to compare people with one another or even to rate them on a scale.

So the emphasis on accountability for past performance started to fade. That continued as jobs became more complex and rapidly changed shape—in that climate, it was difficult to set annual goals that would still be meaningful 12 months later. Plus, the move toward team-based work often conflicted with individual appraisals and rewards. And low inflation and small budgets for wage increases made appraisal-driven merit pay seem futile. What was the point of trying to draw performance distinctions when rewards were so trivial?

The whole appraisal process was loathed by employees anyway. Social science research showed that they hated numerical scores— they would rather be told they were "average" than given a 3 on a

5-point scale. They especially detested forced ranking. As Wharton's Iwan Barankay demonstrated in a field setting, performance actually declined when people were rated relative to others. Nor did the ratings seem accurate. As the accumulating research on appraisal scores showed, they had as much to do with who the rater was (people gave higher ratings to those who were like them) as they did with performance.

And managers hated *doing* reviews, as survey after survey made clear. Willis Towers Watson found that 45% did not see value in the systems they used. Deloitte reported that 58% of HR executives considered reviews an ineffective use of supervisors' time. In a study by the advisory service CEB, the average manager reported spending about 210 hours—close to five weeks—doing appraisals each year.

As dissatisfaction with the traditional process mounted, high-tech firms ushered in a new way of thinking about performance. The "Agile Manifesto," created by software developers in 2001, outlined several key values—favoring, for instance, "responding to change over following a plan." It emphasized principles such as collaboration, self-organization, self-direction, and regular reflection on how to work more effectively, with the aim of prototyping more quickly and responding in real time to customer feedback and changes in requirements. Although not directed at performance per se, these principles changed the definition of effectiveness on the job—and they were at odds with the usual practice of cascading goals from the top down and assessing people against them once a year.

So it makes sense that the first significant departure from traditional reviews happened at Adobe, in 2011. The company was already using the agile method, breaking down projects into "sprints" that were immediately followed by debriefing sessions. Adobe explicitly brought this notion of constant assessment and feedback into performance management, with frequent check-ins replacing annual appraisals. Juniper Systems, Dell, and Microsoft were prominent followers.

CEB estimated in 2014 that 12% of U.S. companies had dropped annual reviews altogether. Willis Towers Watson put the figure at 8% but added that 29% were considering eliminating them or planning to do so. Deloitte reported in 2015 that only 12% of the U.S. companies it surveyed were *not* planning to rethink their performance management systems. This trend seems to be extending beyond the United States as well. PwC reports that two-thirds of large companies in the UK, for example, are in the process of changing their systems.

Three Business Reasons to Drop Appraisals

In light of that history, we see three clear business imperatives that are leading companies to abandon performance appraisals:

The return of people development

Companies are under competitive pressure to upgrade their talent management efforts. This is especially true at consulting and other professional services firms, where knowledge work is the offering—and where inexperienced college grads are turned into skilled advisers through structured training. Such firms are doubling down on development, often by putting their employees (who are deeply motivated by the potential for learning and advancement) in charge of their own growth. This approach requires rich feedback from supervisors—a need that's better met by frequent, informal check-ins than by annual reviews.

Now that the labor market has tightened and keeping good people is once again critical, such companies have been trying to eliminate "dissatisfiers" that drive employees away. Naturally, annual reviews are on that list, since the process is so widely reviled and the focus on numerical ratings interferes with the learning that people want and need to do. Replacing this system with feedback that's delivered right after client engagements helps managers do a better job of coaching and allows subordinates to process and apply the advice more effectively.

Kelly Services was the first big professional services firm to drop appraisals, in 2011. PwC tried it with a pilot group in 2013 and then discontinued annual reviews for all 200,000-plus employees. Deloitte followed in 2015, and Accenture and KPMG made similar announcements shortly thereafter. Given the sheer size of these firms, and the fact that they offer management advice to thousands of organizations, their choices are having an enormous impact on other companies. Firms that scrap appraisals are also rethinking employee management much more broadly. Accenture CEO Pierre Nanterme estimates that his firm is changing about 90% of its talent practices.

The need for agility

When rapid innovation is a source of competitive advantage, as it is now in many companies and industries, that means future needs are continually changing. Because organizations won't necessarily want employees to keep doing the same things, it doesn't make sense to hang on to a system that's built mainly to assess and hold people accountable for past or current practices. As Susan Peters, GE's head of human resources, has pointed out, businesses no longer have clear annual cycles. Projects are short-term and tend to change along the way, so employees' goals and tasks can't be plotted out a year in advance with much accuracy.

At GE a new business strategy based on innovation was the biggest reason the company recently began eliminating individual ratings and annual reviews. Its new approach to performance management is aligned with its FastWorks platform for creating products and bringing them to market, which borrows a lot from agile techniques. Supervisors still have an end-of-year summary discussion with subordinates, but the goal is to push frequent conversations with employees (GE calls them "touchpoints") and keep revisiting two basic questions: What am I doing that I should keep doing? And what am I doing that I should change? Annual goals have been replaced with shorter-term "priorities." As with many of the companies we see, GE first launched a pilot, with about 87,000 employees in 2015, before adopting the changes across the company.

The centrality of teamwork

Moving away from forced ranking and from appraisals' focus on individual accountability makes it easier to foster teamwork. This has become especially clear at retail companies like Sears and Gap—perhaps the most surprising early innovators in appraisals. Sophisticated customer service now requires frontline and back-office employees to work together to keep shelves stocked and manage customer flow, and traditional systems don't enhance performance at the team level or help track collaboration.

Gap supervisors still give workers end-of-year assessments, but only to summarize performance discussions that happen throughout the year and to set pay increases accordingly. Employees still have goals, but as at other companies, the goals are short-term (in this case, quarterly). Now two years into its new system, Gap reports far more satisfaction with its performance process and the best-ever completion of store-level goals. Nonetheless, Rob Ollander-Krane, Gap's senior director of organization performance effectiveness, says the company needs further improvement in setting stretch goals and focusing on team performance.

Implications

All three reasons for dropping annual appraisals argue for a system that more closely follows the natural cycle of work. Ideally, conversations between managers and employees occur when projects finish, milestones are reached, challenges pop up, and so forth—allowing people to solve problems in current performance while also developing skills for the future. At most companies, managers take the lead in setting near-term goals, and employees drive career conversations throughout the year. In the words of one Deloitte manager: "The conversations are more holistic. They're about goals and strengths, not just about past performance."

Perhaps most important, companies are overhauling performance management because their businesses require the change. That's true whether they're professional services firms that must develop people in order to compete, companies that need to deliver ongoing performance feedback to support rapid innovation, or retailers that need better coordination between the sales floor and the back office to serve their customers.

Of course, many HR managers worry: If we can't get supervisors to have good conversations with subordinates once a year, how can we expect them to do so more frequently, without the support of the usual appraisal process? It's a valid question—but we see reasons to be optimistic.

As GE found in 1964 and as research has documented since, it is extraordinarily difficult to have a serious, open discussion about problems while also dishing out consequences such as low merit pay. The end-of-year review was also an excuse for delaying feedback until then, at which point both the supervisor and the employee were likely to have forgotten what had happened months earlier. Both of those constraints disappear when you take away the annual review. Additionally, almost all companies that have dropped traditional appraisals have invested in training supervisors to talk more about development with their employees—and they are checking with subordinates to make sure that's happening.

Moving to an informal system requires a culture that will keep the continuous feedback going. As Megan Taylor, Adobe's director of business partnering, pointed out at a recent conference, it's difficult to sustain that if it's not happening organically. Adobe, which has gone totally numberless but still gives merit increases based on informal assessments, reports that regular conversations between managers and their employees are now occurring without HR's prompting. Deloitte, too, has found that its new model of frequent, informal check-ins has led to more meaningful discussions, deeper insights, and greater employee satisfaction. (For more details, see "Reinventing Performance Management," HBR, April 2015.) The firm started to go numberless like Adobe but then switched to assigning employees several numbers four times a year, to give them rolling feedback on different dimensions. Jeffrey Orlando, who heads up development and performance at Deloitte, says the company has been tracking the effects on business results, and they've been positive so far.

Challenges That Persist

The greatest resistance to abandoning appraisals, which is something of a revolution in human resources, comes from HR itself. The reason is simple: Many of the processes and systems that HR has built over the years revolve around those performance ratings. Experts in employment law had advised organizations to standardize practices, develop objective criteria to justify every employment decision, and

FIGURE 7-1

A talent management timeline

The tug-of-war between accountability and development over the decades

WWI	WWII	1940s	1950s	1960s	1970s
The U.S. military created a merit-rating system to flag and dismiss poor performers.	The army devised forced ranking to identify enlisted soldiers with the potential to become officers.	About 60% of U.S. companies were using appraisals to document workers' performance and allocate rewards.	Social psychologist Douglas McGregor argued for engaging employees in assessments and goal setting.	Led by General Electric, companies began splitting appraisals into separate discussions about accountability and growth, to give development its due.	Inflation rates shot up, and organizations felt pressure to award merit pay more objectively, so accountability again became the priority in the appraisal process.

1980s	1990s	2000	2011	2016
Jack Welch championed forced ranking at GE to reward top performers, accommodate those in the middle, and get rid of those at the bottom.	McKinsey's War for Talent study pointed to a shortage of capable executives and reinforced the emphasis on assessing and rewarding performance.	Organizations got flatter, which dramatically increased the number of direct reports each manager had, making it harder to invest time in developing them.	Kelly Services was the first big professional services firm to drop appraisals, and other major firms followed suit, emphasizing frequent, informal feedback. Adobe ended annual performance reviews, in keeping with the famous "Agile Manifesto" and the notion that annual targets were irrelevant to the way its business operated.	Deloitte, PwC, and others that tried going numberless are reinstating performance ratings but using more than one number and keeping the new emphasis on developmental feedback.

■ Accountability focus
⊡ Development focus
☐ A hybrid "third way"

document all relevant facts. Taking away appraisals flies in the face of that advice—and it doesn't necessarily solve every problem that they failed to address.

Here are some of the challenges that organizations still grapple with when they replace the old performance model with new approaches:

Aligning individual and company goals

In the traditional model, business objectives and strategies cascaded down the organization. All the units, and then all the individual employees, were supposed to establish their goals to reflect and reinforce the direction set at the top. But this approach works only when business goals are easy to articulate and held constant over the course of a year. As we've discussed, that's often not the case these days, and employee goals may be pegged to specific projects. So as projects unfold and tasks change, how do you coordinate individual priorities with the goals for the whole enterprise, especially when the business objectives are short-term and must rapidly adapt to market shifts? It's a new kind of problem to solve, and the jury is still out on how to respond.

Rewarding performance

Appraisals gave managers a clear-cut way of tying rewards to individual contributions. Companies changing their systems are trying to figure out how their new practices will affect the pay-for-performance model, which none of them have explicitly abandoned.

They still differentiate rewards, usually relying on managers' qualitative judgments rather than numerical ratings. In pilot programs at Juniper Systems and Cargill, supervisors had no difficulty allocating merit-based pay without appraisal scores. In fact, both line managers and HR staff felt that paying closer attention to employee performance throughout the year was likely to make their merit-pay decisions more valid.

But it will be interesting to see whether most supervisors end up reviewing the feedback they've given each employee over the year before determining merit increases. (Deloitte's managers already do this.) If so, might they produce something *like* an annual appraisal score—even though it's more carefully considered? And could that subtly undermine development by shifting managers' focus back to accountability?

Identifying poor performers

Though managers may assume they need appraisals to determine which employees aren't doing their jobs well, the traditional process doesn't *really* help much with that. For starters, individuals' ratings jump around over time. Research shows that last year's performance score predicts only one-third of the variance in this year's score— so it's hard to say that someone simply isn't up to scratch. Plus, HR departments consistently complain that line managers don't use the appraisal process to document poor performers. Even when they do, waiting until the end of the year to flag struggling employees allows failure to go on for too long without intervention.

We've observed that companies that have dropped appraisals are requiring supervisors to immediately identify problem employees. Juniper Systems also formally asks supervisors each quarter to confirm that their subordinates are performing up to company standards. Only 3%, on average, are not, and HR is brought in to address them. Adobe reports that its new system has reduced dismissals, because struggling employees are monitored and coached much more closely.

Still, given how reluctant most managers are to single out failing employees, we can't assume that getting rid of appraisals will make those tough calls any easier. And all the companies we've observed still have "performance improvement plans" for employees identified as needing support. Such plans remain universally problematic, too, partly because many issues that cause poor performance can't be solved by management intervention.

Avoiding legal troubles

Employee relations managers within HR often worry that discrimination charges will spike if their companies stop basing pay increases and promotions on numerical ratings, which seem objective. But appraisals haven't prevented discriminatory practices. Though they force managers to systematically review people's contributions each year, a great deal of discretion (always subject to bias) is built into the process, and considerable evidence shows that supervisors discriminate against some employees by giving them undeservedly low ratings.

Leaders at Gap report that their new practices were driven partly by complaints and research showing that the appraisal process was often biased and ineffective. Frontline workers in retail (disproportionately women and minorities) are especially vulnerable to unfair treatment. Indeed, formal ratings may do more to *reveal* bias than to curb it. If a company has clear appraisal scores and merit-pay indexes, it is easy to see if women and minorities with the same scores as white men are getting fewer or lower pay increases.

All that said, it's not clear that new approaches to performance management will do much to mitigate discrimination either. (See the sidebar "Can you take cognitive bias out of assessments?") Gap has found that getting rid of performance scores increased fairness in pay and other decisions, but judgments still have to be made—and there's the possibility of bias in every piece of qualitative information that decision makers consider.

Managing the feedback firehose

In recent years most HR information systems were built to move annual appraisals online and connect them to pay increases, succession planning, and so forth. They weren't designed to accommodate continuous feedback, which is one reason many employee check-ins consist of oral comments, with no documentation.

The tech world has responded with apps that enable supervisors to give feedback anytime and to record it if desired. At General Electric, the PD@GE app ("PD" stands for "performance development") allows managers to call up notes and materials from prior conversations and summarize that information. Employees can use the app to ask for direction when they need it. IBM has a similar app that adds another feature: It enables employees to give feedback to peers and choose whether the recipient's boss gets a copy. Amazon's

Can You Take Cognitive Bias Out of Assessments?

A classic study by Edward Jones and Victor Harris in the 1960s demonstrated that people tend to attribute others' behavior to character rather than circumstances.

When a car goes streaking past us, for instance, we think that the driver is a jerk and ignore the possibility that there might be an emergency. A good workplace example of this cognitive bias—known as the "fundamental attribution error"—is to assume that the lowest performers in any year will always be the worst performers and to fire them as a result. Such an assumption overlooks the impact of good or poor management, not to mention business conditions that are beyond employees' control.

Of course, this model is highly flattering to people who have advanced into executive roles—"A" players whose success is, by definition, credited to their superior abilities, not to good fortune. That may be partly why the model has persisted so long in the face of considerable evidence against it.

Even when "A" players seem to perform well in many contexts (and that's rarely measured), they may be coasting on the "halo effect"—another type of bias, akin to self-fulfilling prophecy. If these folks have already been successful, they receive more opportunities than others, and they're pushed harder, so naturally they do better.

Biases color individual performance ratings as well. Decision makers may give past behavior too much weight, for instance, or fall prey to stereotypes when they assign their ratings.

But when you get rid of forced ranking and appraisal scores, you don't eradicate bias. Discrimination and faulty assumptions still creep into qualitative assessments. In some ways the older, more cumbersome performance systems actually made it harder for managers to keep their blinders on. Formal feedback from various stakeholders provided some balance when supervisors were otherwise inclined to see only the good things their stars did and failed to recognize others' contributions.

Anytime you exercise judgment, whether or not you translate that to numerical ratings, intuition plays a part, and bias can rear its head.

Anytime Feedback tool does much the same thing. The great advantage of these apps is that supervisors can easily review all the discussion text when it is time to take actions such as award merit pay or consider promotions and job reassignments.

Of course, being on the receiving end of all that continual coaching could get overwhelming—it never lets up. And as for peer feedback, it isn't always useful, even if apps make it easier to deliver in real time. Typically, it's less objective than supervisor feedback, as anyone familiar with 360s knows. It can be also "gamed" by employees to help or hurt colleagues. (At Amazon, the cutthroat culture encourages employees to be critical of one another's performance, and forced ranking creates an incentive to push others to the bottom of the heap.) The more consequential the peer feedback, the more likely the problems.

Not all employers face the same business pressures to change their performance processes. In some fields and industries (think sales and financial services), it still makes sense to emphasize accountability and financial rewards for individual performers. Organizations with a strong public mission may also be well served by traditional appraisals. But even government organizations like NASA and the FBI are rethinking their approach, having concluded that accountability should be collective and that supervisors need to do a better job of coaching and developing their subordinates.

Ideology at the top matters. Consider what happened at Intel. In a two-year pilot, employees got feedback but no formal appraisal scores. Though supervisors did not have difficulty differentiating performance or distributing performance-based pay without the ratings, company executives returned to using them, believing they created healthy competition and clear outcomes. At Sun Communities, a manufactured-home company, senior leaders also oppose eliminating appraisals because they think formal feedback is essential to accountability. And Medtronic, which gave up ratings several years ago, is resurrecting them now that it has acquired

Ireland-based Covidien, which has a more traditional view of performance management.

Other firms aren't completely reverting to old approaches but instead seem to be seeking middle ground. As we've mentioned, Deloitte has backpedaled from giving no ratings at all to having project leads and managers assign them in four categories on a quarterly basis, to provide detailed "performance snapshots." PwC recently made a similar move in its client-services practices: Employees still don't receive a single rating each year, but they now get scores on five competencies, along with other development feedback. In PwC's case, the pushback against going numberless actually came from employees, especially those on a partner track, who wanted to know how they were doing.

At one insurance company, after formal ratings had been eliminated, merit-pay increases were being shared internally and then interpreted as performance scores. These became known as "shadow ratings," and because they started to affect other talent management decisions, the company eventually went back to formal appraisals. But it kept other changes it had made to its performance management system, such as quarterly conversations between managers and employees, to maintain its new commitment to development.

It will be interesting to see how well these "third way" approaches work. They, too, could fail if they aren't supported by senior leadership and reinforced by organizational culture. Still, in most cases, sticking with old systems seems like a bad option. Companies that don't think an overhaul makes sense for them should at least carefully consider whether their process is giving them what they need to solve current performance problems and develop future talent. Performance appraisals wouldn't be the least popular practice in business, as they're widely believed to be, if *something* weren't fundamentally wrong with them.

Originally published in October 2016. Reprint R1610D

People Before Strategy

A New Role for the CHRO.

by Ram Charan, Dominic Barton, and Dennis Carey

CEOs KNOW THAT they depend on their company's human resources to achieve success. Businesses don't create value; people do. But if you peel back the layers at the vast majority of companies, you find CEOs who are distanced from and often dissatisfied with their chief human resources officers (CHROs) and the HR function in general. Research by McKinsey and the Conference Board consistently finds that CEOs worldwide see human capital as a top challenge, and they rank HR as only the eighth or ninth most important function in a company. That has to change.

It's time for HR to make the same leap that the finance function has made in recent decades and become a true partner to the CEO. Just as the CFO helps the CEO lead the business by raising and allocating financial resources, the CHRO should help the CEO by building and assigning talent, especially key people, and working to unleash the organization's energy. Managing human capital must be accorded the same priority that managing financial capital came to have in the 1980s, when the era of the "super CFO" and serious competitive restructuring began.

CEOs might complain that their CHROs are too bogged down in administrative tasks or that they don't understand the business. But let's be clear: It is up to the CEO to elevate HR and to bridge any gaps that prevent the CHRO from becoming a strategic partner. After all, it was CEOs who boosted the finance function beyond simple accounting. They were also responsible for creating the marketing function from what had been strictly sales.

Elevating HR requires totally redefining the work content of the chief human resources officer—in essence, forging a new contract with this leader—and adopting a new mechanism we call the G3—a core group comprising the CEO, the CFO, and the CHRO. The result will be a CHRO who is as much a value adder as the CFO. Rather than being seen as a supporting player brought in to implement decisions that have already been made, the CHRO will have a central part in corporate decision making and will be properly prepared for that role.

These changes will drive important shifts in career paths for HR executives—and for other leaders across the company. Moreover, the business will benefit from better management of not just its financial resources but also its human ones. We say this with confidence, based on our experience with companies such as General Electric, BlackRock, Tata Communications, and Marsh, all of which act on their commitment to the people side of their businesses.

The CEO's New Contract with the CHRO

A CFO's job is partly defined by the investment community, the board, outside auditors, and regulators. Not so for the CHRO role—that's defined solely by the CEO. The chief executive must have a clear view of the tremendous contribution the CHRO could be making and spell out those expectations in clear, specific language. Putting things in writing ensures that the CEO and CHRO have a shared understanding of appropriate actions and desirable outputs.

To start redefining the job, the CEO should confer with his or her team and key board members, particularly the board's compensation committee (more aptly called the talent and compensation committee), and ask what they expect in an ideal CHRO. Beyond handling the usual HR responsibilities—overseeing employee satisfaction,

Idea in Brief

The Problem

CEOs consistently rank human capital as a top challenge, but they typically undervalue their chief human resources officer and view HR as less important than other functions.

The Solution

The CHRO must become a true strategic partner to the CEO.

The Approach

The CEO must rewrite the CHRO's job description and create a core decision-making body comprising the CEO, CFO, and CHRO.

workforce engagement, benefits and compensation, diversity, and the like—what should an exemplary CHRO do?

Here are three activities we think are critical: predicting outcomes, diagnosing problems, and prescribing actions on the people side that will add value to the business. Some of these things may seem like the usual charter for a CHRO, but they are largely missing in practice, to the disappointment of most CEOs.

Predicting outcomes

CEOs and CFOs normally put together a three-year plan and a one-year budget. The CHRO should be able to assess the chances of meeting the business goals using his knowledge of the people side. How likely is it, for example, that a key group or leader will make timely changes in tune with rapid shifts in the external environment, or that team members will be able to coordinate their efforts? CHROs should raise such questions and offer their views.

Because a company's performance depends largely on the fit between people and jobs, the CHRO can be of enormous help by crystallizing what a particular job requires and realistically assessing whether the assigned person meets those requirements. Jobs that are high leverage require extra attention. Many HR processes tend to treat all employees the same way, but in our observation, 2% of the people in a business drive 98% of the impact. Although coaching can be helpful, particularly when it focuses on one or two things that are preventing individuals from reaching their potential, it has its limits. Nothing overcomes a poor fit. A wide gap between a leader's talents and the job requirements creates problems for the leader, her boss, her peers, and her reports. So before severe damage is done, the CHRO should take the initiative to identify gaps in behavior or skills, especially among those 2% and as job requirements change.

The CHRO, with the CFO, should also consider whether the key performance indicators, talent assignments, and budgets are the right ones to deliver desired outcomes. If necessary, the pair should develop new metrics. Financial information is the most common basis for incentivizing and assessing performance, because it is easy to measure, but the CHRO can propose alternatives. People should be paid according to how much value they contribute to the company—some combination of the importance of the job and how they handle it. Finance and HR should work together to define ahead of time the value that is expected, using qualitative as well as quantitative factors. Imagine the leaders of those functions discussing a business unit manager and triangulating with the CEO and the group executive to better understand what the manager needs to do to outperform the competition in the heat of battle. For example, to move faster into digitization, will he have to reconstitute the team or reallocate funds? Predicting success means weighing how well-attuned the manager is to outside pressures and opportunities, how resilient he would be if the economy went south, and how quickly he could scale up into digitization. The specific metrics would be designed accordingly.

As another example, a top marketing manager might have to build capability for using predictive data in advertising. The CFO and CHRO should recognize that if the manager fails to steep herself in the fundamentals of data analytics and is slow to hire people with that expertise, new competitors could come in and destroy value for the company. Metrics should reflect how quickly the marketing head acts to reorient her department. One set of metrics would focus on the recruiting plan: What steps must the marketing manager take by when? These become milestones to be met at particular points in time. Another set of metrics might focus on budget allocations: Once the new people are hired and assimilated, is the manager reallocating the marketing budget? And is that money in fact helping to increase revenue, margins, market share in selected segments, or brand recognition? Such improvements are measurable, though with a time lag.

The CHRO should also be able to make meaningful predictions about the competition. Just as every army general learns about his counterpart on the enemy side, the CHRO should be armed with information about competitors and how their key decision makers and executors stack up against those at the CHRO's organization. Predictions should include the likely impact of any changes related to human resources at rival companies—such as modifications to their incentive systems, an increase in turnover, or new expertise they are hiring—and what those changes might signify about their market moves. In 2014, for instance, Apple began to hire medical technology people—an early warning sign that it might make a heavy push to use its watch and perhaps other Apple devices for medical purposes. Such activity could have implications for a health care business, a medical device manufacturer, or a clinic. Similarly, a competitor's organizational restructuring and reassignment of leaders might indicate a sharper focus on product lines that could give your company a tougher run.

Intelligence about competitors is often available through headhunters, the press, employees hired from other companies, suppliers, or customers' customers. Even anecdotal information, such as "The marketing VP is a numbers guy, not a people guy," or "She's a cost cutter and can't grow the business," or "The head of their new division comes from a high-growth company," can improve the power of prediction. For example, Motorola might have been able to anticipate the iPhone if the company's CHRO had alerted the CEO when Apple began trying to recruit Motorola's technical people.

The CHRO should make comparisons unit by unit, team by team, and leader by leader, looking not only at established competitors but also at nontraditional ones that could enter the market. Is the person who was promoted to run hair care at X company more experienced and higher energy than our new division head? Does the development team in charge of wireless sensors at Y company collaborate better than we do? The answers to such questions will help predict outcomes that will show up as numbers on a financial statement sometime in the future.

Diagnosing problems

The CHRO is in a position to pinpoint precisely why an organization might not be performing well or meeting its goals. CEOs must learn to seek such analysis from their CHROs instead of defaulting to consultants.

The CHRO should work with the CEO and CFO to examine the causes of misses, because most problems are people problems. The idea is to look beyond obvious external factors, such as falling interest rates or shifting currency valuations, and to link the numbers with insights into the company's social system—how people work together. A correct diagnosis will suggest the right remedy and avoid any knee-jerk replacements of people who made good decisions but were dealt a bad hand.

If the economy slumped and performance lagged compared to the previous year, the question should be, How did the leader react? Did he get caught like a deer in the headlights or go on the offensive? How fast did he move, relative to the competition and the external change? This is where the CHRO can help make the critical distinction between a leader's misstep and any fundamental unsuitability for the job. Here too the CHRO will learn new things about the leader, such as how resilient he is—information that will be useful in considering future assignments.

But focusing on individual leaders is only half the equation. The CHRO should also be expert at diagnosing how the various parts of the social system are working, systematically looking for activities that are causing bottlenecks or unnecessary friction. When one CEO was reviewing the numbers for an important product line, he saw a decline in market share and profits for the third year in a row. The medical diagnostic product that the group was counting on to reverse the trend was still not ready to launch. As he and his CHRO dug in, they discovered that the marketing team in Milwaukee and the R&D team in France had not agreed on the specifications. On the spot, they arranged a series of face-to-face meetings to resolve the disconnect.

There is great value in having the CHRO diagnose problems and put issues on the table, but such openness is often missing. Behaviors such as withholding information, failing to express disagreement but refusing to take action, and undermining peers often go unnoticed. Some CEOs look the other way rather than tackle conflicts among their direct reports, draining energy and making the whole organization indecisive. Take, for example, problems that arise when collaboration across silos doesn't happen. In such situations, no amount of cost cutting, budget shifting, or admonition will stem the deterioration. Thus CHROs who bring dysfunctional relationships to the surface are worth their weight in gold.

At the same time, the CHRO should watch for employees who are energy creators and develop them. Whether or not they are directly charged with producing results, these are the people who get to the heart of issues, reframe ideas, create informal bonds that encourage collaboration, and in general make the organization healthier and more productive. They may be the hidden power behind the group's value creation.

Prescribing actions to add value

Agile companies know they must move capital to where the opportunities are and not succumb to the all-too-typical imperatives of budgeting inertia ("You get the same funding as last year, plus or minus 5%"). When McKinsey looked at capital allocation patterns in more than 1,600 U.S. companies over 15 years, it found that aggressive reallocators—companies that shifted more than 56% of capital across businesses during that time—had 30% higher total shareholder returns than companies that shifted far less.

Companies should be similarly flexible with their human capital, and CHROs should be prepared to recommend actions that will unlock or create value. These might include recognizing someone's hidden talent and adding that individual to the list of high potentials, moving someone from one position to another to ignite growth in a new market, or bringing in someone from the outside to develop capability in a new technology. Although capital reallocation is important, the reassignment of people along with capital reallocation is what really boosts companies.

Responding to the external environment today sometimes requires leaders with capabilities that weren't previously cultivated, such as knowledge of algorithms, or psychological comfort with digitization and rapid change. The company might have such talent buried at low levels. To have impact, those individuals might need to be lifted three organizational levels at once rather than moved incrementally up existing career ladders. The CHRO should be searching for people who could be future value creators and then thinking imaginatively about how to release their talent. Judging people must be a special skill of the CHRO, just as the CFO has a knack for making inferences from numbers.

Dow Chemical found that aggressively hiring entrepreneurial millennials was the fastest way to create more "short-cycle innovation" alongside the company's traditional long-cycle R&D processes. The share of employees under age 30 went from 9% in 2004 to 15% in 2014. To benefit from this new talent, the company also revamped its career paths to move the 20- and 30-somethings into bigger jobs relatively quickly, and it invited them to global leadership meetings relatively early.

Another way to unlock value is to recommend mechanisms to help an individual bridge a gap or enhance her capacity. These might include moving her to a different job, establishing a council to advise her, or assigning someone to help shore up a particular skill. For example, to build the technology expertise of the small start-ups he funded, the famed venture capitalist John Doerr used his huge relationship network to connect the people running those businesses with top scientists at Bell Labs. In the same vein, CHROs could make better use of their networks with other CHROs to connect people with others who could build their capacity.

The CHRO might also recommend splitting a division into subgroups to unleash growth and develop more P&L leaders. He might suggest particular skills to look for when hiring a leader to run a country unit or big division. Other prescriptions might focus on improving the social engine—the quality of relationships, the level of trust and collaboration, and decisiveness. The CHRO could, for instance, work with business divisions to conduct reviews once a month rather than annually, because reducing the time lag between actions and feedback increases motivation and improves operations.

What not to do

In addition to spelling out clearly what is expected in the way of making predictions, diagnosing problems, and prescribing beneficial actions, the CHRO's new contract should define what she is *not* required to do. This helps provide focus and free time so that she can engage at a higher level. For example, the transactional and administrative work of HR, including managing benefits, could be cordoned off and reassigned, as some companies have begun to do. One option is to give those responsibilities to the CFO. At Netflix, traditional HR processes and routines are organized under the finance function, while HR serves only as a talent scout and coach. Another model we see emerging is to create a shared service function that combines the back-office activities of HR, finance, and IT. This function may or may not report to the CFO.

Compensation has traditionally been the purview of CHROs, but it may be hard for them to appreciate the specific issues business leaders face, just as it is hard for the CFO to understand the nuances of the social engine. Because compensation has such an enormous impact on behavior and on the speed and agility of the corporation, the best solution is for the CEO and CFO to also get involved. While the CHRO can be the lead dog, compensation decisions should be made jointly by the three—and, given the increasingly active role of institutional investors, with the board's engagement.

The CHRO's fit

With a new contract in hand, the chief executive should assess how well the CHRO meets the job specifications now and where he needs to be in three years. Most CHROs have come up through the HR pipeline. While some have had line jobs, most have not; Korn Ferry research indicates that only 40 of the CHROs at *Fortune* 100 companies had significant work experience outside HR before they came to lead that function. This might leave a gap in terms of predicting, diagnosing, and prescribing actions that will improve business performance. However, inclusion in broader discussions will expand a CHRO's understanding of the business. CEOs should give their CHRO a chance to grow into the newly defined role, and they should assess progress quarter by quarter.

Measuring the performance of the CHRO has long been problematic. HR leaders are usually judged on accomplishments such as installing a new process under budget, recruiting a targeted number of people from the right places, or improving retention or employee engagement. Yet such efforts are not directly tied to value creation. In keeping with recasting HR as a value creator rather than a cost center, performance should be measured by outputs that are more closely linked to revenue, profit margin, brand recognition, or market share. And the closer the linkage, the better.

A CHRO can add value by, for example, moving a key person from one boss to another and improving his performance; arranging for coaching that strengthens a crucial skill; bringing a person from the outside into a pivotal position; putting two or three people together to create a new business or initiative to grow the top or bottom line; reassigning a division manager because she will not be able to meet the challenge two years out; or discovering and smoothing friction where collaboration is required. Such actions are observable, verifiable, and closely related to the company's performance and numbers.

Here's a case in point: When a promising young leader was put in charge of three divisions of a large company, replacing an executive vice president with long tenure, the divisions took off. The new EVP, who was growth-oriented and digitally savvy, seized on commonalities among the three businesses in technology and production and nearly halved the product development cycle time. In three years the divisions overtook the competition to become number one.

Creating a G3

To make the CHRO a true partner, the CEO should create a triumvirate at the top of the corporation that includes both the CFO and the CHRO. Forming such a team is the single best way to link financial numbers with the people who produce them. It also signals to the organization that you are lifting HR into the inner sanctum and that the CHRO's contribution will be analogous to the CFO's. Although some companies may want the CHRO to be part of an expanded group that includes, say, a chief technology officer or chief risk officer, the G3, as we call it, is the core group that should steer the company, and it should meet apart from everyone else. The G3 will shape the destiny of the business by looking forward and at the big picture while others bury their heads in operations, and it will ensure that the company stays on the rails by homing in on any problems in execution. It is the G3 that makes the connection between the organization and business results.

At Marsh, a global leader in insurance brokerage and risk management, CEO Peter Zaffino often has one-on-one discussions with his CFO, Courtney Leimkuhler, and his CHRO, Mary Anne Elliott. In April 2015 he held a meeting with both of them to assess the alignment of the organization with desired business outcomes. The G3 began this meeting by selecting a business in the portfolio and drawing a vertical line down the middle of a blank page on a flip chart. The right side was for the business performance (Leimkuhler's expertise); the left side for organizational design issues (Elliott's expertise). A horizontal line created boxes for the answers to two simple questions: What is going well? What is not going well?

"Peter could have filled in the entire two-by-two chart on his own," Elliott says, "but doing it together really added value." Zaffino adds, "The whole meeting took about 15 minutes. We found the exercise to be very worthwhile. We already run the business with disciplined processes. We conduct deep dives into the organization's financial performance through quarterly operational reviews, and we conduct quarterly talent reviews, where we focus on the human capital side. So you might not think we'd want to introduce another process to evaluate how we are managing the business. But this G3 process provided us with a terrific lens into the business without adding bureaucracy."

Working together to synthesize disparate data points into one flip chart helped the team identify items on the organizational side that would predict business performance in the next four to eight quarters. Significant value came from the dialogue as connections emerged naturally. Zaffino says, "We constantly drill down deep to understand why a business is performing the way it is. In those instances, we are drilling vertically, not horizontally, when there could be some items identified on the organizational side that are actually driving the performance." Zaffino cited the implementation of a new sales plan, which HR was working on, as one example. His concern was making sure business results were aligned with remuneration "so we didn't have sales compensation becoming disconnected from the overall financial result of the business," he explains. "We also didn't want to drive top-line growth without knowing how to invest back in the business and increase profitability." The CHRO was thinking it through from her perspective: Is this sales plan motivating the right behaviors so that it moves business performance to the "going well" category?

Seeing the interconnections also helped the trio identify what mattered most. "It's easy enough to list everything we want to do better," Leimkuhler says, "but it's hard to know where to start. When you understand which things on the organizational side are really advancing business performance, it makes it easier to prioritize." For example, managing the transition of regional business leaders was a big issue for HR—one that, because of its difficulty, would have been easy to push off. Seeing the extent to which inaction could be holding back business performance created a greater sense of urgency.

"In the HR world, we talk about understanding and integrating with the business," Elliott notes. "G3 meetings are a pragmatic activity. When you're sitting with the CEO and CFO, there's no place for academic HR. It's all about understanding what the organization needs to do to drive business performance and how to align those key variables."

"There's something to be said for peeling off into a smaller group," Leimkuhler adds. "It would be unwieldy to have this discussion with the full executive committee, which at Marsh consists of 10 executives. In any case, it's not one or the other; it's additive." Says Zaffino, "This was a streamlined way to get a holistic view of the business. Each of us left the first G3 meeting feeling comfortable that the organization and the business were aligned and that we have a very good handle on the business."

Vinod Kumar, CEO of Tata Communications, also uses an informal G3 mechanism. Kumar's company supplies communication, computing, and collaboration infrastructure to large global companies, including many telephone and mobile operators. In 2012 there were price drops of 15% to 20%, and disruptive technologies were par for the course. To keep pace, Tata Communications had to transform its business very quickly, which meant building critical new capabilities by hiring from the outside, at least in the short term— an effort that would hardly help the company deal with rising costs. Something had to give, and Kumar enlisted then-CFO Sanjay Baweja and CHRO Aadesh Goyal to help chart a path forward while taking into account both financial and talent considerations.

Frequent discussions among the G3 led to a consensus: Tata Communications would restructure roles that had become redundant or were out of sync with the company's new direction, and it would move jobs to the right geographical locations. These actions would reduce staffing costs by 7%. The company would use the savings to build the necessary capabilities, mainly by making new hires, especially in sales, marketing, and technology.

The G3 next went to work on changes that would occur over a longer time. Tata Communications launched a companywide program in late 2013 aimed at continuously improving productivity. The initial objective was to reduce the cost base by $100 million, but the overall intention was to seed a new culture. The G3 began by creating a cross-functional team that employees joined part-time. Ultimately more than 500 people participated, working on ideas in

50 categories and achieving even more cost reductions than originally targeted. In short, the project was a big success, and it continues to produce results.

Dialogue—both institutionalized and informal—between the CHRO, the CFO, and the CEO is now a way of life at Tata Communications. In time, as CHRO Goyal's grasp of the business became evident, Kumar made a bold move: He gave Goyal the additional responsibility of managing one of the company's high-growth subsidiaries and made him part of the Innovation Council, which identifies opportunities to invest in and incubate new businesses.

Regular G3 Meetings

If a G3 is to be effective, the CEO has to ensure that the triumvirate meets on a regular basis.

Weekly temperature taking

The CEO, CFO, and CHRO should get together once a week to discuss any early warning signals they are picking up internally or externally about the condition of the social engine. Each of them will see things through a different lens, and pooling their thoughts will yield a more accurate picture. The three don't have to be together physically—they can arrange a conference call or video chat—but meeting frequently is important. After about six weeks, and with discipline, such sessions could be finished in 15 to 20 minutes.

The CEO has to set the tone for these reviews, ensuring that the discussion is balanced and that intellectual honesty and integrity are absolute. It's a given that both the CFO and the CHRO must be politically neutral to build trust, and they must never sacrifice their integrity to be the CEO's henchmen. They must be willing to speak up and tell it like it is. Over time, each G3 member will have a better understanding of the others' cognitive lenses, discussions will be more fluid, and all three will learn a lot about the intricacies of the business. They will also become more comfortable correcting one another's biases, more skilled at reading people, and more likely to get the right people in the right jobs.

Looking forward monthly

The G3 should spend a couple of hours every month looking four and eight quarters ahead with these questions in mind: What people issues would prevent us from meeting our goals? Is there a problem with an individual? With collaboration? Is a senior team member unable to see how the competition is moving? Is somebody likely to leave us?

Companies do operational reviews, which are backward-looking, at least quarterly. The objective here is to be predictive and diagnostic, looking forward not just at the numbers but also at the people side, because most failures and missed opportunities are people-related. There may be organizational issues, energy drains, or conflicts among silos, particularly in the top two layers. Conflicts are inherent in matrix organizations; the G3 needs to know where they exist, whether they could affect progress on a new initiative, and how the leaders in charge are handling them. Probing such matters is not micromanagement or a witch hunt. It's a means of finding the real causes of both good and poor performance and taking corrective action promptly or preemptively.

Planning three years out

It is common practice to plan where the company needs to be in three years and to decide what new projects to fund and where to invest capital. Often missing from that process is exploration of the people questions: Will we have employees with the right skills, training, and temperament to achieve the targets? Will our people have the flexibility to adapt to changing circumstances? In most strategic planning, there is zero consideration of the critical players in the organization—or those working for competitors.

Discussion of people should come before discussion of strategy. (This is a practice that General Electric is known for.) What are employees' capabilities, what help might they need, and are they the very best? The CEO and the CHRO of one company decided that for every high-leverage position that opened, they should have five candidates—three from inside, two from outside. Talent should always be viewed in a broad context. Consider who is excelling, being let go, or being lured away, along with any other information that could affect your competitiveness or your rivals'.

New HR Leadership Channels

Some CEOs might be holding back on elevating their CHROs because they lack confidence in the HR leader's business judgment and people acumen. There's a fear that HR chiefs aren't prepared to discuss issues beyond hiring, firing, payroll, benefits, and the like. That reservation must be met head-on by providing rich opportunities for CHROs to learn. Give them more exposure to the business side through meetings of the G3, and provide some coaching. If knowledge or skills gaps persist, ask the CHRO how she might fill them. Some CHROs will rise to the occasion. Others won't measure up, and the supply of suitable replacements might be scarce at first. (The same issue applied in the 1980s to finding the right CFO types from the ranks of accounting.)

An enduring solution is to create new career paths for HR leaders to cultivate business smarts and for business leaders to cultivate people smarts. Every entry-level leader, whether in HR or some other job, should get rigorous training in judging, recruiting, and coaching people. And those who begin their careers in HR leadership should go through rigorous training in business analysis, along the lines of what McKinsey requires for all its new recruits. There should be no straight-line leadership promotions up the functional HR silo. Aspiring CHROs should have line jobs along the way, where they have to manage people and budgets.

All leaders headed for top jobs should alternate between positions in HR and in the rest of the business. Make it a requirement for people in the top three layers of the company to have successfully worked as an HR leader, and the function will soon become a talent magnet. Be sure that it isn't just ticket punching. Those who have no feel for the people side are unlikely to succeed for long in high-level jobs.

The Transition to the New HR

Any CEO who is sold on the idea that people are the ultimate source of sustainable competitive differentiation must take the rejuvenation and elevation of the HR function very seriously. Creating a mechanism that knits the CFO and the CHRO together will improve the business and expand the CEO's personal capability. It won't happen overnight—three years seems to us the minimum time required to achieve a shift of this magnitude. Stating the new expectations for the CHRO and the human resources function is a good place to begin. Creating ways to blend business and people acumen should follow. And redesigning career tracks and talent reviews will take the company further still. But none of this will happen unless the CEO personally embraces the challenge, makes a three-year commitment, and starts executing.

Originally published in July–August 2015. Reprint R1507D

Toward a Racially Just Workplace

by Laura Morgan Roberts and Anthony J. Mayo

"**SUCCESS IS TO BE MEASURED** not so much by the position that one has reached in life as by the obstacles which [one] has overcome while trying to succeed."

Booker T. Washington, the educator, author, activist, and presidential adviser, wrote those words more than a century ago as a way of encouraging his African American compatriots—many of them recently emancipated from slavery—to persist in the fight for equal rights and economic opportunities. He was proud of what he and his peers had achieved. He surely believed there was satisfaction in struggling against and surmounting bad odds. And yet we must also assume that he, along with millions of other freedom fighters, wanted future generations of Black Americans to suffer fewer hardships. He hoped today's Black leaders would find easier paths to success.

Has that dream been realized? Having spent the past 20 years conducting and reviewing research on African Americans' advancement, particularly in the workplace, and having collected our work and others' into a book, we must report that the answer is partly yes but mostly no.

No doubt, there has been progress. Civil rights laws have been passed and affirmed. Companies are committing to and investing heavily in diversity, because more corporate leaders acknowledge that it makes good business sense. And several Black billionaires and CEOs sit on the respective ranking lists.

However, according to both quantitative and qualitative data, working African Americans—from those laboring in factories and on shop floors to those setting C-suite strategy—still face obstacles to advancement that other minorities and white women don't. They are less likely than their white peers to be hired, developed, and promoted. And their lived experience at work is demonstrably worse even than that of other people of color.

These challenges might, as Washington said, make success sweeter for the few who overcome them. But a huge gap remains between what organizations are saying and doing to promote inclusion and the outcomes we're seeing for many Black workers and managers. If leaders want to walk their talk, they must spearhead much more meaningful change. Instead of undervaluing and squandering Black talent, they must recognize the resilience, robust sense of self, and growth mindset that, studies show, African American people—as one of the most historically oppressed groups in the United States—bring to the table. They should work even harder to seek out and support them, from entry-level recruitment to CEO succession.

We have not identified any major company that is doing this well on a broad scale. But research and lessons gleaned from other contexts can point the way forward. In our work with leading management thinkers and practitioners across the country, we have arrived at a four-step strategy to help companies move toward greater and better representation for Black leaders. It involves shifting from an exclusive focus on the business case for racial diversity to embracing the moral one, promoting real conversations about race, revamping diversity and inclusion programs, and better managing career development at every stage. Given the increasing importance of purpose and social impact to employees, customers, and other stakeholders, we believe there's no better time to make this transformation. We also believe our framework can be adapted for other marginalized groups in the United States and around the world.

Taking these steps won't be easy; executives will need to think deeply about their ethics and corporate culture and exert extra effort

Idea in Brief

At most large U.S. and multinational organizations, diversity and inclusion have become imperatives, but African Americans' progress remains slow. Even worse is the lived experience of Black employees, who often feel like outsiders—and are tempted to walk out the door. Laura Morgan Roberts and Anthony J. Mayo argue that organizations should take specific steps toward racial justice:

- Shift from an exclusive focus on the most lucrative thing to do to the right thing to do.

- Encourage open conversations about race.

- Revamp diversity and inclusion programs to clarify goals and focus on proactive steps.

- Manage career development across all life stages, from campus recruitment to the consideration of Black executives for top jobs.

These steps won't be easy, but maximizing the human potential of everyone in the workplace is the ultimate reward.

for a cause they may not consider central to their business. But the reward will be great: maximizing the human potential of everyone in the workplace.

Underrepresented, Unsupported, Unfulfilled

At most large U.S. and multinational organizations, diversity and inclusion (D&I) has become an imperative. Companies are pushing for minority recruitment, paying for antibias training, and sponsoring nonwhite employees for high-potential leadership-development programs. Research has shown, and a great many executives now understand, that a heterogeneous workforce yields more innovation and better performance than a homogeneous one does.

And yet 55 years after the passage of the Civil Rights Act and decades into these corporate D&I efforts, African Americans' progress toward top management roles and greater economic well-being and influence remains slow to nonexistent. Let's look first at the demographics.

The Big Idea: Advancing Black Leaders

"Toward a Racially Just Workplace" is the lead article of HBR's **The Big Idea: Advancing Black Leaders**. You can read the rest of the series at hbr.org/blackleaders:

- "The Costs of Code-Switching," by Courtney L. McCluney, Kathrina Robotham, Serenity Lee, Richard Smith, and Myles Durkee

- "The Day-to-Day Work of Diversity and Inclusion," by Paige Cohen and Gretchen Gavett

- "Why So Many Organizations Stay White," by Victor Ray

- "Success Comes from Affirming Your Potential," by Laura Morgan Roberts and Anthony J. Mayo

What the numbers say

Yes, we can point to the rise of several prominent Black leaders, from media figures Oprah Winfrey, Robert Johnson, and Jay-Z to financiers Ken Chenault and Robert Smith and sports-stars-turned-businesspeople Serena Williams, Michael Jordan, and LeBron James. Most notably, America elected its first African-descended president, Barack Obama, in 2008 and reelected him in 2012. The number of African Americans earning bachelor's and graduate degrees continues to increase. And Black people account for 12% of the U.S. workforce, close to their 13.4% representation in the general population.

However, in the words of leaders from the Toigo Foundation, a career advancement organization for underrepresented groups, such evidence merely gives us "the illusion of inclusion." In fact, research shows that in the United States, the wealth gap between Blacks and others continues to widen; experts predict that Black families' median wealth will decrease to $0 by 2050, while that of white families will exceed $100,000. Just 8% of managers and 3.8% of CEOs are Black. In the *Fortune* 500 companies, there are currently only three Black chief executives, down from a high of 12 in 2002. And at the 16 *Fortune* 500 companies that report detailed demographic data on senior executives and board members, white men account for 85% of those roles.

Black leaders have struggled to make inroads in a variety of influential industries and sectors. At U.S. finance companies, only 2.4% of executive committee members, 1.4% of managing directors, and 1.4% of senior portfolio managers are Black. A mere 1.9% of tech executives and 5.3% of tech professionals are African American. Black representatives and senators account for 9% of the U.S. Congress. The average Black partnership rate at U.S. law firms from 2005 to 2016 was 1.8%. Only 7% of U.S. higher education administrators and 8% of nonprofit leaders are Black. And just 10% of U.S. businesses are owned by Black men and women. As the Toigo Foundation points out, all this has a cascading impact on economic development, housing, jobs, quality of schools and other services, access to education, infrastructure spending, consumer credit, retirement savings, and more.

What it's like at work
Underrepresentation is bad enough. But even worse, according to extensive research, is the lived experience of Black employees and managers in the U.S. workplace. African Americans continue to face both explicit racism—stoked by the rise of white nationalism in the past few years—and subtle racism on the job. In the latter category, University of Utah professor emeritus Arthur Brief points to "aversive" racism (when people avoid those of different races or change their behavior around them) along with "modern" racism (when people believe that because Blacks can now compete in the marketplace, they no longer face discrimination). Microaggressions—for example, when a white male visitor to an office assumes that a Black female executive is a secretary—are also common.

Although companies claim they want to overcome these explicit and implicit biases and hire and promote diverse candidates, they rarely do so in effective ways. When Harvard Business School's emeriti professors David A. Thomas and John Gabarro conducted an in-depth six-year study of leaders in three companies, they found that people of color had to manage their careers more strategically than their white peers did and to prove greater competence before winning promotions. And research by Lynn Perry Wooten, the dean of Cornell University's Dyson School, and Erika Hayes James, the dean of Emory University's Goizueta Business School, shows that Black leaders who do rise to the top are disproportionately handed "glass cliff" assignments, which offer nice rewards but carry a greater risk of failure. Other research, such as Duke University professor Ashleigh Rosette's studies of Black leaders, has shown widespread racial differences in hiring, performance ratings, promotions, and other outcomes.

There is also an emotional tax associated with being Black in the American workplace. Research by the University of Virginia's Courtney McCluney and Catalyst's Dnika Travis and Jennifer Thorpe-Moscon shows that because Black employees feel a heightened sense of difference among their mostly white peers, their ability to contribute is diminished. "The sense of isolation, of solitude, can take a toll," one leader told them. "It's like facing each day with a core of uncertainty . . . wondering . . . if the floor you're standing on is concrete or dirt . . . solid or not."

Many Black professionals have reported to Toigo that they are expected to be "cultural ambassadors" who address the needs of other Black employees, which leaves them doing two jobs: "the official one the person was hired to do, and a second one as champion for members of the person's minority group," as one put it. Across industries, sectors, and functions, they also experience the "diversity fatigue" that arises from constantly engaging in task forces, trainings, and conversations about race as they are tapped to represent their demographic.

And Black leaders in particular struggle with feeling inauthentic at work. Research by McGill University's Patricia Faison Hewlin shows that many minorities feel pressured to create "facades of conformity," suppressing their personal values, views, and attributes to fit in with organizational ones. But as Hewlin and her colleague Anna-Maria Broomes found in a survey of 2,226 workers in various industries and corporate settings, African Americans create these facades more frequently than other minority groups do and feel the inauthenticity more deeply. They might chemically relax (straighten) their hair, conform with coworkers' behavior, "whitewash" their résumés by deleting ethnic-sounding names or companies, hide minority beliefs, and suppress emotions related to workplace racism.

As a result of all the above, Black workers feel less supported, engaged, and committed to their jobs than their non-Black peers do, as research from Georgetown University's Ella Washington, Gallup's Ellyn Maese and Shane McFeely, and others has documented. Black managers report receiving less psychosocial support than their white counterparts do. Black employees are less likely than whites or Hispanics to say that their company's mission or purpose makes them feel that their job is important, that their coworkers will do quality work, and that they have opportunities to learn and grow. Black leaders are more likely than white ones to leave their organizations. It's clear that the norms and cultural defaults of leadership in most organizations create an inhospitable environment that leaves even those Black employees who have advanced feeling like outsiders—and in some cases pushes them out the door.

Relatively high pay and impressive pedigrees don't help much: According to a survey of diverse professionals with bachelor's or graduate degrees and average annual incomes of $100,000 or more that one of us (Laura) conducted with colleagues at the Partnership, a nonprofit organization specializing in diversity and leadership development, African Americans report the lowest levels of both manager and coworker support, commitment, and job fit and the highest levels of feeling inauthentic and wanting to leave their jobs. Studies of Black Harvard Business School and Harvard Law School graduates have similarly found that matriculating from highly respected institutions does not shield one from obstacles. When surveyed years and even decades after graduating, Black Harvard MBAs expressed less satisfaction than their white counterparts with opportunities to do meaningful work, to realize professional accomplishments, and to combine career with personal and family life. "Perhaps it sounds naive, but [coming out of HBS] I did not expect race to have any bearing in my career," one told us. "I was wrong."

Leading Change

As we said earlier, diversity and inclusion efforts have been gaining traction, and workforces are becoming increasingly multiracial. But given the dearth of Black leaders, we would like to see companies jump-start their efforts in four ways.

First, move away from the business case and toward a moral one

The dozens of D&I executives we talked to in the course of our research tell us they sometimes feel they've taken the business case for diversity as far as it can go. When Weber Shandwick surveyed 500 chief diversity officers at companies with revenue of $500 million or more, results confirmed that proving that ROI—showing that inclusive teams yield more-creative ideas that appeal to broader customer bases, open new markets, and ultimately drive better performance—is one of the biggest challenges.

The research on this is clear. A 2015 McKinsey report on 366 public companies found that those in the top quartile for ethnic and racial diversity in management were 35% more likely than others to have financial returns above the industry mean. Various studies have shown that teams composed of both white and Black people are more likely to focus on facts, carefully process information, and spur innovation when the organizational culture and leadership support learning across differences.

With the right knowledge, skills, and experience, African American employees and managers can add as much business value as anyone else. They may have greater insights about creating and selling offerings for minority consumer groups that end up appealing to white consumers as well. As one of us (Tony) showed in research with Nitin Nohria, now the dean of Harvard Business School, and Eckerd College's Laura Singleton, some of the most successful Black entrepreneurs are those who—in some cases *because* they were marginalized—built companies to serve their same-race peers, particularly in the personal care, media, and fashion arenas. Examples include the 19th-century Black-hair-care trailblazer Madam C. J. Walker, Black Entertainment Television's

Robert and Sheila Johnson, and Daymond John, who launched the FUBU clothing line.

So, experts agree that diversity enhances business outcomes when managed well. But given the limited progress African Americans have made in most of corporate America, it seems clear that the sound business arguments for inclusion are not enough. At many companies, D&I executives still struggle for airtime in the C-suite and for resources that can move their organizations beyond the tokenism of, say, one Black executive in the senior ranks. Their business cases don't appear to have been as persuasive as those presented by their marketing, operations, and accounting colleagues, which have a more direct effect on the bottom line.

And in more-progressive companies—ones truly committed to inclusion—a different kind of pushback sometimes occurs: If a team incorporates women, Asians, Latinos, and representatives of the LGBTQ community alongside white men, if it has data geeks and creative types, extroverts and introverts, Harvard MBAs and college dropouts, able-bodied and physically challenged members, isn't it diverse enough? Our answer: Not when teams, especially those at the highest levels, leave out the most marginalized group in the United States.

Thus we turn to the moral case. Many in the U.S. business community have begun to push for a more purpose-driven capitalism that focuses not just on shareholder value but also on shared value—benefits that extend to employees, customers, suppliers, and communities. This movement, toward what the University of Toronto's Sarah Kaplan calls the 360° Corporation, wants corporate leaders to consider both the financial and the ethical implications of all their decisions. We believe that one of its pillars should be proportionate representation and wages for Black Americans.

Why this group in particular? As the *New York Times*'s excellent 1619 Project highlighted, we are exactly four centuries away from the start of slavery—the kidnapping, forced labor, mistreatment, and often murder of African people—in the United States. And we are just 154 years away from its end. Although discrimination based on race and other factors was outlawed by the Civil Rights Act of 1964, the effects of slavery and the decades of discrimination and disenfranchisement that followed it continue to hold back many descendants of enslaved people (and those from different circumstances who have the same skin color). Alarmingly, racism and racist incidents are on the rise: According to the FBI, the number of hate crimes committed in the United States rose by 17% from 2016 to 2017, marking the third consecutive year of increases.

We also can't forget that a compelling business case can be—and has been—made for all the atrocities listed above. Indeed, when invoked absent humanistic and ethical principles, a "business case" has legitimated exploitative actions throughout history. White landowners argued that the economic welfare of the colonies and the health of a young country depended on keeping Black people in chains. White business owners in the Jim Crow South and segregated neighborhoods across the country claimed that sales would suffer if Black customers and residents—who in the absence of land and good jobs had amassed little wealth—were allowed in, because that would turn rich white customers away. And white executives have long benefited because people of color with less access to high-quality education and high-wage employment were forced into low-paying commercial and household jobs, from coal mining and call center work to cleaning, cooking, and caregiving.

So the case for racial diversity and the advancement of African Americans can't be solely about increasing innovation or providing access to and legitimacy in minority markets to maximize revenue and profits. We can't simply ask, "What's the most lucrative thing to do?" We must also ask, "What's the right thing to do?" The imperative should be creating a context in which people of all colors, but especially those who have historically been oppressed, can realize their full potential. This will involve exploring and understanding the racist history that has shaped various groups' access to resources and opportunities and that undergirds contemporary bias. It means emphasizing equity and justice.

How might this work? Starbucks has made some attempts. In the wake of protests following the 2014 fatal shooting of Michael Brown by police in Ferguson, Missouri, the coffee chain announced RaceTogether, which aimed to spark a national conversation about race relations by having baristas write that phrase on customers' cups. The campaign fell flat because it was perceived more as a profit-minded marketing stunt than as a good-faith effort to change the status quo. Subsequent initiatives, perhaps designed with ethics more squarely in mind, have garnered a more positive response. In 2015 Starbucks launched a hiring program to recruit disadvantaged youths, including African Americans; in 2017 it expanded that program and added one to recruit refugees; and after a racially charged incident at one of its cafés in 2018, it closed all its U.S. cafés for a day of employee antibias training. Consider, too, Nike's decision to launch a marketing campaign headlined by Colin Kaepernick, the NFL quarterback who failed to get picked up by a team after he began kneeling during the national anthem to protest the unfair treatment of African Americans. The campaign created a backlash among anti-Kaepernick consumers and a #BoycottNike hashtag, but the sports apparel brand stood by its tagline: "Believe in something. Even if it means sacrificing everything." We applaud these steps and hope organizations will go even further in learning how to practice racial inclusion in their workplaces.

Some organizations have invoked the moral case for action in other contexts. Think of how Patagonia supports environmental protections by committing to donate either 1% of sales or 10% of profits (whichever is larger) to advocacy groups. And recall that Dick's Sporting Goods pulled assault weapons and high-capacity magazines from its stores following the Parkland, Florida, school shooting, even though it projected—accurately—that the move would mean a $250 million hit to sales. (It's important to note that over the long term, none of those companies suffered from their choices.)

Such stances take courage. But by combining the business case and the moral one, leaders can make a more powerful argument for supporting Black advancement.

Second, encourage open conversations about race
As Dartmouth College's Ella Bell and the University of Pretoria's Stella Nkomo note in the introduction to our book, "Organizations are in society, not apart from it." And although President Obama's election brought some talk of a post-racial era in the United States,

the stories and statistics that have come out in the past few years show that racism still exists, which means that race still matters and needs to be discussed, candidly and frequently, in the workplace.

Those conversations will not immediately feel comfortable. Research shows that although many people are happy to talk about "diversity" or "inclusion," their enthusiasm drops significantly when the subject is "race." Most of us don't like to think very hard about where minorities sit and what power they wield (or don't) within our organizations—much less discuss it. When we examine who has been excluded in what ways over what period of time, the concept of white privilege might come up. And majority-group employees might express concerns about reverse discrimination. (According to an Ernst & Young study of 1,000 U.S. workers, one-third of respondents said that a corporate focus on diversity has overlooked white men.) Charged topics like these can provoke resentment, anger, and shame. But we need real exchanges about them if we want to dispel the notion that corporations are pure meritocracies and to ensure that everyone feels heard, supported, and authentic at work.

Senior leaders—most of whom are white men—must set the tone. Why? In one survey, nearly 40% of Black employees said they feel it is *never* acceptable to speak out about experiences of bias—a silence that can become corrosive. Another study showed that among Black professionals who aspire to senior leadership positions, the most frequently adopted strategy is to avoid talking about race or other issues of inequality, for fear of being labeled an agitator. Other research has indicated that the only CEOs and lower-level managers not penalized for championing diversity are white men.

To create a culture of psychological safety and pave the way for open communication will require a top-down directive and modeling through informal and formal discussions in which people are asked to share ideas, ask questions, and address issues without fear of reprisal. Managers down the line will need training in encouraging and guiding such exchanges, including inviting Black employees and leaders to share their experiences—the good, the bad, and the ugly. Participants should be trained to prepare for such conversations by reflecting on their own identities and the comments and situations that trigger strong emotions in them. As detailed by Columbia University's Valerie Purdie-Greenaway and the University of Virginia's Martin Davidson, the goal is to shift the entire organization to a racial-learning orientation.

Again, a movement from another context—#MeToo—sheds light on how to do so. Revelations of abuse and harassment and the out-pouring of women's stories that followed, many about incidents that happened in the workplace, forced corporate leaders to focus on those issues. Bad actors were fired, women felt empowered to speak up, and awareness of gender discrimination increased. Although #BlackLivesMatter has had similar success highlighting and sparking discussions around police brutality, there is no #BlackLivesAtWork. There should be.

We see some positive signs on this front. Over the past few years several prominent leaders, including PwC's Tim Ryan, Interpublic Group's Michael Roth, Kaiser Permanente's Bernard Tyson, and AT&T's Randall Stephenson, have initiated companywide discussions of race. For example, PwC brought in Mellody Hobson, president and co-CEO of Ariel Investments and a prominent African American leader, to talk to employees about being "color-brave" instead of "color-blind" at work, and it has offered guides for continuing the discussion. At Morgan Stanley, global head of D&I Susan Reid has promoted intimate conversations about race in networking groups and an hour-long forum on race in the current social climate. The latter was moderated by the company's vice chairman and featured its chief marketing officer, its head of prime brokerage, and a *Fortune* reporter who covers racial issues; it was attended by 1,500 employees, and videos of the event were shared across the firm. Greenaway and Davidson also point to a mostly white male financial services firm that instituted Know Us, a program of small-group cross-race dialogues on racially relevant topics.

Over time these conversations will start to happen informally and organically in groups and among individuals at all levels of an organization, deepening interpersonal cross-race relationships. In one consulting company cited by Greenaway and Davidson, non-Black employees started a book club open to all but focused on Black writers; the group has visited African American museums and historical sites. One-on-one interactions can be even more meaningful, as the psychologist colleagues Karen Samuels (who is white) and Kathryn Fraser (who is Black) describe. "It was important to name our racial and cultural differences and to examine how my perspective was naive regarding her reality," Samuels explains.

Third, revamp D&I programs

Any corporate diversity and inclusion program is better than none, but most that exist today are not designed to sustain a focus on racial equity. Many are siloed within the HR department, lack C-suite support, or are given to women or people of color to manage in addition to their day jobs. Some are more show than go, resting on philosophical statements about inclusion rather than outlining concrete steps for advancing nonwhites. Others limit their efforts to antibias and cultural competence training—preempting problems but, again, not propelling anyone forward. Most take a broad-brush approach to diversity, attempting to serve all minorities plus white women, LGBTQ employees, and those who are neurodiverse or disabled and offering uniform training and leadership development that ignore historical patterns of exclusion, marginality, and disadvantage for each group. They might focus too heavily on recruitment and retention—filling the pipeline and high-potential groups with Black employees but failing to support them past middle-management roles. Most troubling, as Courtney McCluney and San Francisco State University's Verónica Rabelo have shown, a significant portion of D&I programs try to "manage Blackness"—that is, impose "desirable" and "professional" (read: white) norms and expectations on rising African American stars, thus preserving rather than shifting the status quo. They train Black executives to fit into the existing organizational culture rather than encourage them to broaden it by bringing their true and most productive selves to work.

How can we improve such programs? By tackling their shortcomings one by one. Here are several steps organizations can take.

- Give D&I sustained C-suite support and recognize and reward the people who contribute to its initiatives—for example, by having your chief diversity officer report directly to the CEO and tracking inclusion initiative participation in performance reviews and promotion and pay raise discussions.

- Equip and invite white men to take up the mantle—say, by bringing them into D&I programs and assigning some of them to leadership roles.

- Challenge those running D&I efforts to set clear goals for how representation, organizational networks, and access to resources should change across functions and levels over time and how Black employees' perceptions, engagement, and well-being should improve, and then measure the efforts' effectiveness with data analysis and qualitative surveys.

- Shift from preventive measures, such as antibias training, to proactive ones, such as upping the number of Black candidates considered for open positions and stretch roles.

- Abandon one-size-fits-all and color-blind leadership-development practices in favor of courses and coaching tailored to specific groups—or better yet, adopt personalized plans that recognize the multifaceted nature of each individual.

- Help Black employees and rising leaders throughout their careers, including teaching managers the skills they need to support D&I efforts.

- Stop asking Black employees to blend in; instead, emphasize the value of a workplace that embraces all styles and behaviors.

In sum, D&I needs to be an ethos that permeates the entire organization, championed not just by the HR department but by everyone, and especially managers, so that its importance is clear. The Toigo Foundation's leaders draw a parallel between this idea and the total quality management movement of the 1980s, which, with top-down support and the establishment of key performance indicators, became a pervasive way of working and thinking that filtered down to every function and level.

Few companies to date have taken diversity and inclusion that far. But some are moving in the right direction, including JPMorgan Chase, which in 2016 launched a board- and CEO-supported Advancing Black Leaders strategy—staffed and managed separately from other D&I initiatives—focused on filling the firm's pipeline with Black talent and retaining and promoting those workers. SAP's Black Employee Network helped launch its partnership with Delaware State University through Project Propel, which offers tech training and skills development to students from historically Black colleges and universities (HBCUs), with the goal of building an employee pipeline. The Network also encouraged SAP to sponsor Silicon Valley's Culture Shifting Weekend, which brings together more than 200 African American and Hispanic executives, entrepreneurs, innovators, and social impact leaders to discuss diversifying the tech industry. Pfizer tracks numerous D&I metrics and notes that 21% of its workforce—21,000 people—are actively involved in its D&I efforts.

Finally, manage career development across all life stages

African Americans today are securing good university educations in record numbers. HBCUs, in particular, create a sizable pipeline of young talent for organizations to tap into. Companies can, of course, step up their campus recruiting efforts, but efforts to advance Black leaders must extend far beyond that.

If more African Americans are to rise through the ranks, robust—and careful—investment in retention and development is required. Research by the University of Georgia's Kecia Thomas and colleagues has shown that many Black women get this kind of support early in their careers, but it comes with a price: They are treated like "pets" whom white leaders are happy to groom, but the further they progress, the more that favored status begins to undermine them. Those who reject the pet identity, meanwhile, are perceived as threatening and face hostility and distancing from coworkers.

Mentoring is useful, and our study of Black HBS graduates shows that they were more likely than their white peers to have been formally assigned to mentors. But they derived less value from the relationship and said that informal mentorship—having senior executives (white or minority) connect with them naturally through work groups or common interests—was more effective. "A mentor helps you navigate the power structure of the firm, especially when there is no one in senior management who looks like you," one study participant told us.

Early in their careers, Black employees need safe spaces to grow and develop and to experience authentic failures and successes without being subsumed in narratives of racial limitation. Managers and mentors can provide the necessary cover. We found that the Black Harvard MBAs who did reach top management positions (13% of women, 19% of men) had been bolstered by networks of supporters.

Sponsorship—that is, recommending Black employees for promotions and stretch assignments—is even more important. Other key factors that have propelled Black Harvard MBAs into senior executive roles are line or general management experience and global assignments. With many qualified and ambitious people vying for such opportunities, politics often plays a role. So African Americans need more influential people in their corners, pressing their cases to decision-makers.

Candid feedback early on is also critical. This doesn't mean pushing protégés to assimilate (to look and act "more white"); as we've shown, that's counterproductive. It should focus on identifying and enhancing their unique strengths, overcoming skill or knowledge weaknesses, and positioning them to realize their full potential.

At later stages of their careers, Black executives should be seriously considered for high-stakes and high-profile positions and supported in the pursuit of outside interests, such as board seats, that enhance visibility. And while taking care not to tokenize but rather to create opportunities for multiple candidates, organizations can highlight those executives as role models who redefine norms of leadership and can encourage them to pass that baton by transferring connections and endorsements, sharing wisdom through storytelling, and creating opportunities for the next generation to assume senior roles. Needs differ by career stage, a fact that most published models of diversity and inclusion do not address but that is embedded in impactful programs such as the Toigo Foundation, the Partnership, and the Executive Leadership Council.

Despite antidiscrimination laws and increasing corporate investment in diversity efforts, race continues to be a major barrier to advancement in the U.S. workplace. We are far from realizing the principles of equal opportunity and meritocracy. Rather than looking to the few Black leaders who have succeeded as exemplars of exceptionalism who have beaten almost insurmountable odds, we must learn from their insights and experiences along with the experiences of those who didn't make it to the top. Perhaps more important, we need to understand why existing inclusion initiatives have made so little difference. If organizations really want a representative workforce that includes more than one or two Black leaders, their approach must change.

Our hope is that once companies understand the reality of the Black experience, they will embrace and champion policies and programs that actually help to level the playing field—and that where there aren't yet best practices, they will begin the conversations and experiments that will lead to them. This will be hard and often uncomfortable work. But we believe it's worth it, not only for African Americans but also for the many other underrepresented or marginalized groups. Now more than ever before, organizations and society should strive to benefit from the experiences, knowledge, and skills of all, not just a few. And while government policies can help, we believe that corporate leaders can have a much more powerful and immediate impact. As then-Senator Obama said in 2008, *"Change will not come if we wait for some other person or if we wait for some other time. We are the ones we've been waiting for. We are the change that we seek."*

Originally published in November 2019. Reprint BG1906

How to Do Hybrid Right

by Lynda Gratton

BY LATE FEBRUARY 2020, as the implications of Covid-19 were becoming clear, Hiroki Hiramatsu, the head of global HR at Fujitsu, realized that the company was in for a shock.

For years, flexible work arrangements had been on the agenda at Fujitsu, but little had actually changed. Most managers in the Japan offices still prized face-to-face interaction and long office hours—and according to an internal survey conducted not long before, more than 74% of all employees considered the office to be the best place to work. But the pandemic, Hiramatsu foresaw, was about to turn everything upside down.

By the middle of March, the majority of Fujitsu's Japan-based employees—some 80,000—were working from home. And it didn't take long for them to appreciate the advantages of their new flexibility. By May, according to a follow-up survey, only 15% of Fujitsu employees considered the office to be the best place to work. Some 30% said the best place was their homes, and the remaining 55% favored a mix of home and office—a hybrid model.

As employees settled into their new routines, Hiramatsu recognized that something profound was happening. "We are not going back," he told me this past September. "The two hours many people spend commuting is wasted—we can use that time for education, training, time with our family. We need many ideas about how to make remote work effective. We are embarking on a work-life shift."

For 10 years, I've led the Future of Work Consortium, which has brought together more than 100 companies from across the world to research future trends, identify current good practice, and learn from emerging experiments. Since the pandemic I've focused our research on the extraordinary impact that Covid-19 is having on working arrangements. As part of that effort, I've talked extensively to executives, many of whom, like Hiramatsu, report that they've detected a silver lining in our collective struggle to adapt to the pandemic. These executives told me that given the astonishing speed with which companies have adopted the technology of virtual work, and the extent to which most employees don't want to revert to past ways of working, they're seeing a once-in-a-lifetime opportunity to reset work using a hybrid model—one that, if we can get it right, will allow us to make our work lives more purposeful, productive, agile, and flexible.

If leaders and managers want to make this transition successfully, however, they'll need to do something they're not accustomed to doing: design hybrid work arrangements with individual human concerns in mind, not just institutional ones.

The Elements of Hybrid

Figuring out how to do this is far from straightforward. That's because to design hybrid work properly, you have to think about it along two axes: place and time.

Place is the axis that's getting the most attention at the moment. Like Fujitsu's employees, millions of workers around the world this year have made a sudden shift from being place-constrained (working in the office) to being place-unconstrained (working anywhere). Perhaps less noticed is the shift many have also made along the time axis, from being time-constrained (working synchronously with others) to being time-unconstrained (working asynchronously whenever they choose).

To help managers conceptualize the two-dimensional nature of this problem, I've long used a simple 2x2 matrix that's organized along those axes. (See the exhibit "Work arrangements in place and time.") Before Covid-19, most companies offered minimal flexibility

Idea in Brief

The Opportunity

Since the pandemic, companies have adopted the technologies of virtual work remarkably quickly—and employees are seeing the advantages of more flexibility in where and when they work. As companies recognize what is possible, they are embracing a once-in-a-lifetime opportunity to reset work using a hybrid model.

The Challenge

Moving to an anywhere, anytime hybrid model will succeed only if it is designed with human concerns in mind, not just institutional ones.

The Way Forward

That requires companies to approach the problem from four different perspectives: (1) jobs and tasks, (2) employee preferences, (3) projects and workflows, and (4) inclusion and fairness.

along both dimensions. This put them in the lower-left quadrant, with employees working in the office during prescribed hours. Some firms had begun to venture into the lower-right quadrant, by allowing more-flexible hours; others were experimenting in the upper-left quadrant, by offering employees more flexibility in where they work, most often from home. Very few firms, however, were moving directly into the upper-right quadrant, which represents an anywhere, anytime model of working—the hybrid model.

But that's changing. As we emerge from the pandemic, many companies have firmly set their sights on flexible working arrangements that can significantly boost productivity and employee satisfaction. Making that happen, I've learned in my research, will require that managers consider the challenge from four distinct perspectives: (1) jobs and tasks, (2) employee preferences, (3) projects and workflows, and (4) inclusion and fairness. Let's look at each in turn.

Jobs and Tasks

When thinking about jobs and tasks, start by understanding the critical drivers of productivity—energy, focus, coordination, and cooperation—for each. Next, consider how those drivers will be affected by changes in working arrangements along the axes of time and place.

To illustrate, let's consider a few kinds of jobs and tasks, their key drivers, and the time and place needs that each involves:

Strategic planner

A critical driver of productivity for this role is focus. Planners often need to work undisturbed for stretches of at least three hours in order to, for example, gather market information and develop business plans. The axis that best enables focus is time—specifically, asynchronous time. If planners are freed from the scheduled demands of others, place becomes less critical: They can perform their work either at home or in the office.

Team manager

Here the critical driver of productivity is coordination. Managers need to regularly communicate in-the-moment feedback with team members. They need to engage in conversation and debate, share best practices, and mentor and coach those on their team. The axis most likely to encourage this aspect of productivity is once again time—but in this case, the time needs to be synchronous. If that can be arranged, then place again becomes less critical: Managers and employees can do their coordination tasks together in the office or from home, on platforms such as Zoom and Microsoft Teams.

Product innovator

For this role, the critical driver is cooperation. But now the important axis is place. Innovation is stimulated by face-to-face contact with colleagues, associates, and clients, who generate ideas in all sorts of ways: by brainstorming in small groups, bumping into one another in the hallways, striking up conversations between meetings, attending group sessions. This kind of cooperation is fostered most effectively in a shared location—an office or a creative hub where employees have the chance to get to know one another and socialize. To that end, cooperative tasks must be synchronous and

FIGURE 10-1

Work arrangements in place and time

Working in the office from 9 to 5 used to be the norm, with companies allowing limited flexibility in where or when employees worked. The pandemic has upended that model, as managers recognize that many employees can work productively anywhere, anytime.

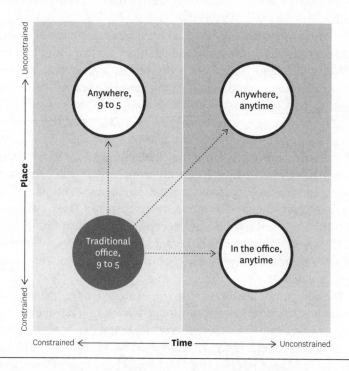

conducted in a shared space. Looking to the future, we can expect that the development of more-sophisticated cooperative technologies will render shared physical space less of an issue.

Marketing manager

Productivity in this role—indeed, in most roles—requires sustained energy. Both time and place can play a role here. As we've learned during the pandemic, many people find being at home energizing, because they are freed from the burden of long commutes, they can take time out during the day to exercise and walk, they can eat more healthily, and they can spend more time with their families.

The challenge in designing hybrid work arrangements is not simply to optimize the benefits but also to minimize the downsides and understand the trade-offs. Working from home can boost energy, but it can also be isolating, in a way that hinders cooperation. Working on a synchronous schedule can improve coordination, but it can also introduce constant communications and interruptions that disrupt focus.

To combat these potential downsides, Hiramatsu and his team at Fujitsu have committed to creating an ecosystem of spaces that together make up what they call the borderless office. Depending on employees' or teams' specific drivers of productivity, these spaces can take several forms: hubs, which maximize cooperation; satellites, which facilitate coordination; and shared offices, which enable focus.

Fujitsu's hubs are designed with cross-functional cooperation and serendipitous encounters in mind. Located in the major cities, they are comfortable and welcoming open-plan spaces, equipped with the advanced technologies necessary for brainstorming, team building, and the cocreation of new products. When Fujitsu employees want to work creatively with customers or partners, they invite them to a hub.

The company's satellites are spaces designed to facilitate coordination within and between teams that are working on shared projects. They contain meeting spaces where teams can come together, both in person and virtually, supported by secure networks and advanced videoconferencing facilities. These opportunities for coordination, especially face-to-face, address some of the isolation and loneliness that employees may suffer when working from home.

Shared offices, which make up most of Fujitsu's ecosystem of spaces, are located all over Japan, often near or in urban or suburban train stations. They can be used as short stopovers when people are traveling to visit customers, or as alternatives to working at home. They are designed to function as quiet spaces that employees can easily get to, thus minimizing commuting time. The productivity aim here is focus. The shared offices are equipped with desks and internet connections, allowing employees to work independently and undisturbed or to attend online meetings or engage in online learning.

Employee Preferences

Our capacity to operate at peak productivity and performance varies dramatically according to our personal preferences. So in designing hybrid work, consider the preferences of your employees—and enable others to understand and accommodate those preferences.

Imagine, for example, two strategic planners who hold the same job at the same company, with focus as a critical driver of performance. One of them, Jorge, is 40. He and his family live some distance from his office, requiring him to commute an hour each day to and from work. He has a well-equipped home office, and his children are at school during the day—so, not surprisingly, Jorge feels he is most productive and focused when he can skip the commute and stay home alone to work. He prefers to go into the office only once or twice a week, to meet with his team.

Lillian's situation is very different. She's 28. She lives in the center of town and shares a small apartment with three other people. Because of her living situation, she can't work for long stretches of time at home without being disturbed. To focus, she prefers to be in the office, which is not far from where she lives.

Jorge and Lillian differ in another way: tenure with the company. This, too, affects their preferences. Jorge has been with the firm for eight years and has established a strong network, so time in the office is less crucial for his learning or development. Lillian, on the other hand, is new to her role and is keen to be mentored and coached, activities that demand time with others in the office.

Companies on the hybrid journey are finding ways to take their employees' perspective. Many, like one of the technology companies in the Future of Work Consortium, are providing managers with simple diagnostic survey tools to better understand their teams' personal preferences, work contexts, and key tasks—tools that allow them to learn, for example, where their team members feel most energized, whether they have a well-functioning home office, and what their needs are for cooperation, coordination, and focus.

Equinor, a Norwegian energy company, has recently taken an ingenious approach to understanding its employees: It surveyed them about their preferences and developed nine composite "personas," with guidelines for hybrid work arrangements tailored to each one. One of the personas is described like this: "Anna" is a sector manager in Oslo who has been with the company for 20 years. She has three teenagers at home and a 40-minute bicycle commute into the office. Before Covid-19, she worked every other week from home, primarily to focus. But with her teenagers now doing remote schooling in the house, she is often distracted when working from home. When the pandemic is at last behind us, and her kids are back at school, she hopes to spend two days a week at home, doing focused work, and three days in the office, collaborating with her team.

As managers seek to identify the hybrid arrangements that are best for their teams, they consider, for example, how they would respond to an "Anna": How would her circumstances and preferences affect her capacity to collaborate with others? More broadly, managers consider the implications of coordinating a variety of personas across virtual teams. What are the risks to the safety, security, and effectiveness of operations? How will changes affect collaboration, leadership, and culture? What might the overall effects be when it comes to taxes, compliance, and external reputation?

Projects and Workflows

To make hybrid a success, you have to consider how work gets done. An executive who manages Jorge and Lillian, the hypothetical strategic planners mentioned above, must not only consider their needs and preferences but also coordinate the work they do with that of the others on their team—and with other functions and consumers of their work. That kind of coordination was relatively straightforward when team members all worked in the same place at the same time. But in the era of hybrid work it has grown significantly more complex. I've observed executives tackling this in two ways.

One is to significantly boost the use of technology to coordinate activities as employees move to more-flexible work arrangements. Consider the case of Jonas, an Equinor employee. Jonas works as an inspection engineer in the Kollsnes plant, which processes gas from fields in the North Sea. After the pandemic hit, the plant's managers made it possible for Jonas and his team to carry out some inspection tasks from home, by supplying them with state-of-the-art video and digital tools. These include, for example, robotic devices that move around the plant recording detailed in-the-moment visual data, which is then streamed back to all the team members for analysis. As a result of these changes, Jonas and his colleagues can now conduct very effective remote field-safety inspections.

Managers at Fujitsu, for their part, use a range of digital tools to categorize and visualize the types of work their teams are performing as they experiment with new arrangements on the axes of time and place. That, in turn, has enabled them to better assess individual and team workloads, analyze remote working conditions, and confirm work projections. Team leaders are also able to understand employee working patterns by studying detailed movement data and examining space utilization and floor density data. This allows Fujitsu managers to design the right arrangements for their workflows and projects.

Other companies are using this moment as an opportunity to reimagine workflows. New hybrid arrangements should never replicate existing bad practices—as was the case when companies began automating work processes, decades ago. Instead of redesigning their workflows to take advantage of what the new technologies made possible, many companies simply layered them onto existing processes, inadvertently replicating their flaws, idiosyncrasies, and workarounds. It often was only years later, after many painful rounds of reengineering, that companies really began making the most of those new technologies.

Companies designing hybrid arrangements need to work hard to get workflows right the first time. Leaders at one of the retail banks in our Future of Work Consortium analyzed and reimagined work-flows by asking three crucial questions:

Are any team tasks redundant? When executives at the bank asked themselves that question, they realized that in their new hybrid model they had retained too many traditional meetings. By eliminating some and making others (such as status updates) asynchronous, they boosted productivity.

Can any tasks be automated or reassigned to people outside the team? In many new hybrid arrangements, the bank executives realized, the simple answer was yes. Take the process for opening an account with a new high-net-worth customer. Before Covid-19, everybody assumed that this required face-to-face meetings and client signatures. But now, thanks to the redesigned process introduced during the pandemic, bank managers and customers alike recognize the ease and value of remote sign-up.

Can we reimagine a new purpose for our place of work? Here, too, the answer turned out to be yes. To make their hybrid model work successfully, the bank executives decided to reconfigure their existing office space in ways that would encourage cooperation and creativity, and they invested more in tools to enable people to work effectively and collaboratively at home.

Inclusion and Fairness

As you develop new hybrid practices and processes, pay particular attention to questions of inclusion and fairness. This is vitally important. Research tells us that feelings of unfairness in the workplace can hurt productivity, increase burnout, reduce collaboration, and decrease retention.

In the past, when companies began experimenting with flexible approaches to work, they typically allowed individual managers to drive the process on an ad hoc basis. As a result, different departments and teams were afforded varying degrees of flexibility and freedom, which inevitably gave rise to accusations of unfairness. And many employees, of course, had time- and place-dependent jobs that made hybrid arrangements either impossible or far from optimal. They often felt treated unfairly.

Brit Insurance has done admirable work on inclusion and fairness. As the company's CEO, Matthew Wilson, and its chief engagement officer, Lorraine Denny, began the design and implementation of new ways of working, early in 2020, they made a bold choice. Rather than involving "the usual suspects" in the design process, they randomly chose employees from offices in the United States, Bermuda, and London—amounting to 10% of the workforce, from receptionists to senior underwriters—to participate.

During the following six months, teams of six employees—each drawn from multiple divisions, levels, and generational cohorts—worked together virtually across Brit Insurance. They began with diagnostic tools that helped them profile and share their own working capabilities and preferences. Then they embarked on a series of learning modules designed to create deeper insights into how they could work together to better serve one another's needs and those of the company as a whole. Finally, they engaged in a half-day virtual "hackathon," during which they came up with ideas and pitched them to the CEO. The result was what they called the Brit Playbook, which described some of the new ways they would now all work together.

Selina Millstam, the vice president and head of talent management at Ericsson, a Swedish multinational, recently conducted a similarly inclusive effort. Every new work arrangement, she and the executive team decided, would have to be rooted in the company culture, important aspects of which were "a speak-up environment," "empathy," and "cooperation and collaboration."

To ensure that this would be the case, Millstam and her team last year engaged employees in "jams" that were conducted virtually during a 72-hour period and supported by a team of facilitators, who subsequently analyzed the conversational threads. One of these jams, launched in late April 2020, played a crucial role in giving Ericsson employees a platform to talk about how hybrid ways of working during the pandemic might affect the company culture. More than

17,000 people from 132 countries participated in this virtual conversation. Participants made some 28,000 comments, addressing how working during the pandemic had created both challenges (such as lack of social contact) and benefits (such as increased productivity through reduced distraction).

This jam and others like it helped Ericsson's senior leaders develop a more nuanced understanding of the issues and priorities they need to take into account as they design hybrid work arrangements. Change, they realized, is bound to create feelings of unfairness and inequity, and the best way to address that problem is to ensure that as many employees as possible are involved in the design process. They need to have their voices heard, to hear from others, and to know that the changes being made are not just the result of individual managers' whims and sensibilities.

So how can you propel your firm toward an anywhere, anytime model? Start by identifying key jobs and tasks, determine what the drivers of productivity and performance are for each, and think about the arrangements that would serve them best. Engage employees in the process, using a combination of surveys, personas, and interviews to understand what they really want and need. This will differ significantly from company to company, so don't take shortcuts. Think expansively and creatively, with an eye toward eliminating duplication and unproductive elements in your current work arrangements. Communicate broadly so that at every stage of your journey everybody understands how hybrid arrangements will enhance rather than deplete their productivity. Train leaders in the management of hybrid teams, and invest in the tools of coordination that will help your teams align their schedules.

Finally, ask yourself whether your new hybrid arrangements, whatever they are, accentuate your company's values and support its culture. Carefully and thoughtfully take stock: In the changes you've made, have you created a foundation for the future that everybody in the company will find engaging, fair, inspiring, and meaningful?

Originally published in May–June 2021. **Reprint** R2103C

Your Workforce Is More Adaptable Than You Think

by Joseph Fuller, Judith K. Wallenstein, Manjari Raman, and Alice de Chalendar

MANY MANAGERS HAVE LITTLE FAITH in their employees' ability to survive the twists and turns of a rapidly evolving economy. "The majority of people in disappearing jobs do not realize what is coming," the head of strategy at a top German bank recently told us. "My call center workers are neither able nor willing to change."

This kind of thinking is common, but it's wrong, as we learned after surveying thousands of employees around the world. In 2018, in an attempt to understand the various forces shaping the nature of work, Harvard Business School's Project on Managing the Future of Work and the Boston Consulting Group's Henderson Institute came together to conduct a survey spanning 11 countries—Brazil, China, France, Germany, India, Indonesia, Japan, Spain, Sweden, the United Kingdom, and the United States—gathering responses from 1,000 workers in each. In it we focused solely on the people most vulnerable to changing dynamics: lower-income and middle-skills workers. The majority of them were earning less than the average household income in their countries, and all of them had no more than two years of postsecondary education. In each of eight countries—Brazil, China, France, Germany, India, Japan, the

United Kingdom, and the United States—we then surveyed at least 800 business leaders (whose companies differed from those of the workers we surveyed). In total we gathered responses from 11,000 workers and 6,500 business leaders.

What we learned was fascinating: The two groups perceived the future in significantly different ways. Given the complexity of the changes that companies are confronting today and the speed with which they need to make decisions, this gap in perceptions has serious and far-reaching consequences for managers and employees alike.

Predictably, business leaders feel anxious as they struggle to marshal and mobilize the workforce of tomorrow. In a climate of perpetual disruption, how can they find and hire employees who have the skills their companies need? And what should they do with people whose skills have become obsolete? The CEO of one multinational company told us he was so tormented by that last question that he had to seek counsel from his priest.

The workers, however, didn't share that sense of anxiety. Instead, they focused more on the opportunities and benefits that the future holds for them, and they revealed themselves to be much more eager to embrace change and learn new skills than their employers gave them credit for.

The Nature of the Gap

When executives today consider the forces that are changing how work is done, they tend to think mostly about disruptive *technologies*. But that's too narrow a focus. A remarkably broad set of forces is transforming the nature of work, and companies need to take them all into account.

In our research we've identified 17 forces of disruption, which we group into six basic categories. (See the sidebar "The forces shaping the future of work.") Our surveys explored the attitudes that business leaders and workers had toward each of them. In their responses, we were able to discern three notable differences in the ways that the two groups think about the future of work.

Idea in Brief

The Problem

As they try to build a workforce in a climate of perpetual disruption, business leaders worry that their employees can't—or just won't—adapt to the big changes that lie ahead. How can companies find people with the skills they will need?

What the Research Shows

Harvard Business School and the BCG Henderson Institute surveyed thousands of business leaders and workers around the world and discovered an important gap in perceptions: Workers are far more willing and able to embrace change than their employers assume.

The Solution

This gap represents an opportunity. Companies need to start thinking of their employees as a reserve of talent and energy that can be tapped by providing smart on-the-job skills training and career development.

The first is that *workers seem to recognize more clearly than leaders do that their organizations are contending with multiple forces of disruption, each of which will affect how companies work differently.* When asked to rate the impact that each of the 17 forces would have on their work lives, using a 100-point scale, the employees rated the force with the strongest impact 15 points higher than the force with the weakest impact. In comparison, there was only a nine-point spread between the forces rated the strongest and the weakest by managers.

In fact, the leaders seemed unable or unwilling to think in differentiated ways about the forces' potential for disruption. When asked about each force, roughly a third of them described it as having a significant impact on their organization today; close to half projected that it would have a significant impact in the future; and about a fifth claimed it would have no impact at all. That's a troubling level of uniformity, and it suggests that most leaders haven't yet figured out which forces of change they should make a priority.

Interestingly, workers appeared to be more aware of the opportunities and challenges of several of the forces. Notably, workers focused on the growing importance of the gig economy, and they ranked "freelancing and labor-sharing platforms" as the third most

The Forces Shaping the Future of Work

Accelerating Technological Change

- New technologies that replace human labor, threatening employment (such as driverless trucks)
- New technologies that augment or supplement human labor (for example, robots in health care)
- Sudden technology-based shifts in customer needs that result in new business models, new ways of working, or faster product innovation
- Technology-enabled opportunities to monetize free services (such as Amazon web services) or underutilized assets (such as personal consumption data)

Growing Demand for Skills

- General increase in the skills, technical knowledge, and formal education required to perform work
- Growing shortage of workers with the skills for rapidly evolving jobs

Changing Employee Expectations

- Increased popularity of flexible, self-directed forms of work that allow better work-life balance
- More widespread desire for work with a purpose and opportunities to influence the way it is delivered (for example, greater team autonomy)

---

significant of all 17 forces. Business leaders, however, ranked that force as the least significant.

The second difference that emerged from our survey was this: *Workers seem to be more adaptive and optimistic about the future than their leaders recognize.*

The conventional wisdom, of course, is that workers fear that technology will make their jobs obsolete. But our survey revealed that to be a misconception. A majority of the workers felt that advances such as automation and artificial intelligence would have a positive impact on their future. In fact, they felt that way about

Shifting Labor Demographics

- Need to increase workforce participation of underrepresented populations (such as elderly workers, women, immigrants, and rural workers)

Transitioning Work Models

- Rise of remote work
- Growth of contingent forms of work (such as on-call workers, temp workers, and contractors)
- Freelancing and labor-sharing platforms that provide access to talent
- Delivery of work through complex partner ecosystems (involving multiple industries, geographies, and organizations of different sizes), rather than within a single organization

Evolving Business Environment

- New regulation aimed at controlling technology use (for example, "robot taxes")
- Regulatory changes that affect wage levels, either directly (such as minimum wages or Social Security entitlements) or indirectly (such as more public income assistance or universal basic income)
- Regulatory shifts affecting cross-border flow of goods, services, and capital
- Greater economic and political volatility as members of society feel left behind

two-thirds of the forces. What concerned them most were the forces that might allow *other workers*—temporary, freelance, outsourced—to take their jobs.

When asked why they had a positive outlook, workers most commonly cited two reasons: the prospect of better wages and the prospect of more interesting and meaningful jobs. Both automation and technology, they felt, heralded opportunity on those fronts—by contributing to the emergence of more-flexible and self-directed forms of work, by creating alternative ways to earn income, and by making it possible to avoid tasks that were "dirty, dangerous, or dull."

In every country workers described themselves as more willing to prepare for the workplace of the future than managers believed them to be (in Japan, though, the percentages were nearly equal). Yet when asked what was holding workers back, managers chose answers that blamed employees, rather than themselves. Their most common response was that workers feared significant change. The idea that workers might lack the support they needed from employers was only their fifth-most-popular response.

That brings us to our third finding: *Workers are seeking more support and guidance to prepare themselves for future employment than management is providing.*

In every country except France and Japan, significant majorities of workers reported that they—and not their government or their employer—were responsible for equipping themselves to meet the needs of a rapidly evolving workplace. That held true across age groups and for both men and women. But workers also felt that they had serious obstacles to overcome: a lack of knowledge about their options; a lack of time to prepare for the future; high training costs; the impact that taking time off for training would have on wages; and, in particular, insufficient support from their employers. All are barriers that management can and should help workers get past.

What Employers Can Do to Help

The gap in perspectives is a problem because it leads managers to underestimate employees' ambitions and underinvest in their skills. But it also shows that there's a vast reserve of talent and energy companies can tap into to ready themselves for the future: their workers.

The challenge is figuring out how best to do that. We've identified five important ways to get started.

1. Don't just set up training programs—create a learning culture
If companies today engage in training, they tend to do it at specific times (when onboarding new hires, for example), to prepare

workers for particular jobs (like selling and servicing certain products), or when adopting new technologies. That worked well in an era when the pace of technological change was relatively slow. But advances are happening so quickly and with such complexity today that companies need to shift to a continuous-learning model—one that repeatedly enhances employees' skills and makes formal training broadly available. Firms also need to expand their portfolio of tactics beyond online and off-line courses to include learning on the job through project staffing and team rotations. Such an approach can help companies rethink traditional entry-level barriers (among them, educational credentials) and draw from a wider talent pool.

Consider what happens at Expeditors, a *Fortune* 500 company that provides global logistics and freight-forwarding services in more than 100 countries. In vetting job candidates, Expeditors has long relied on a "hire for attitude, train for skill" approach. Educational degrees are appreciated but not seen as critical for success in most roles. Instead, for all positions, from the lowest level right up to the C-suite, the company focuses on temperament and cultural fit. Once on staff, employees join an intensive program in which every member of the organization, no matter how junior or senior, undertakes 52 hours of incremental learning a year. This practice supports the company's promote-from-within culture. Expeditors' efforts seem to be working: Turnover is low (which means substantial savings in hiring, training, and onboarding costs); retention is high (a third of the company's 17,000 employees have worked at the company for 10 years or more); most senior leaders in the company have risen through the ranks; and several current vice presidents and senior vice presidents, along with the current and former CEOs, got their jobs despite having no college degree.

2. Engage employees in the transition instead of herding them through it

As companies transform themselves, they often find it a challenge to attract and retain the type of talent they need. To succeed, they have to offer employees pathways to professional and personal improvement—and must engage them in the process of change, rather than merely inform them that change is coming.

That's what ING Netherlands did in 2014, when it decided to reinvent itself. The bank's goal was ambitious: to turn itself into an agile institution almost overnight. The company's current CEO, Vincent van den Boogert, recalls that the company's leaders began by explaining the *why* and the *what* of the transformation to all employees. Mobile and digital technologies were dramatically altering the market, they told everybody, and if ING wanted to meet the expectations of customers, improve operations, and deploy new technological capabilities, it would have to become faster, leaner, and more flexible. To do that, they said, the company planned to make investments that would reduce costs and improve service. But it would also eliminate a significant number of jobs—at least a quarter of the total workforce.

Then came the *how*. Rather than letting the ax fall on select employees—a process that creates psychological trauma throughout a company—ING decided that almost everybody at the company, regardless of tenure or seniority, would be required to resign. After that, anybody who felt his or her attitude, capabilities, and skills would be a good fit at the "new" bank could apply to be rehired. That included Van den Boogert himself. Employees who did not get rehired would be supported by a program that would help them find jobs outside ING.

None of this made the company's transformation easy, of course. But according to Van den Boogert, the inclusive approach adopted by management significantly minimized the pain that employees felt during the transition, and it immediately set the new, smaller bank on the path to success. The employees who rejoined ING actively embraced its new mission, felt less survivor's remorse, and devoted themselves with excitement to the job of transformation. "When you talk about the *why, what,* and *how* at the same time," Van den Boogert told us, "people are going to challenge the *why* to prevent the *how*. But in this case, everyone had already been inspired by the *why* and *what*."

3. Look beyond the "spot market" for talent

Most successful companies have adopted increasingly aggressive strategies for finding critical high-skilled talent. Now they must expand that approach to include a wider range of employees. AT&T recognized that need in 2013, while developing its Workforce 2020 strategy, which focused on how the company would make the transition from a hardware-centric to a software-centric network.

The company had undergone a major transformation once before, in 1917, when it launched plans to use mechanical switchboards rather than human operators. But it carried that transformation out over the course of five decades! The Workforce 2020 transformation was much more complex and had to happen on a much faster timeline.

To get started, AT&T undertook a systematic audit of its quarter of a million employees to catalog their current skills and compare those with the skills it expected to need during and after its revamp. Ultimately, the company identified 100,000 employees whose jobs were likely to disappear, and several areas in which it would face skills and competency shortages. Armed with those insights, the company launched an ambitious, multiyear $1 billion initiative to develop an internal talent pipeline instead of simply playing the "spot market" for talent. In short, to meet its evolving needs, AT&T decided to make retraining available to its existing workforce. Since then, its employees have taken nearly 3 million online courses designed to help them acquire skills for new jobs in fields such as application development and cloud computing.

Already, this effort has yielded some unexpected benefits. The company now hires far fewer contractors to meet its needs for technical skills, for example. "We're shifting to employees," one of the company's top executives told CNBC this past March, "because we're starting to see the talent inside."

4. Collaborate to deepen the talent pool

In a fast-evolving environment, competing for talent doesn't work. It simply leads to a tragedy of the commons. Individual companies try to grab the biggest share of the skilled labor available, and these self-interested attempts just end up creating a shortage for all.

To avoid that problem, companies will have to fundamentally change their outlook and work together to ensure that the talent pool is constantly refreshed and updated. That will mean teaming up with other companies in the same industry or region to identify relevant skills, invest in developing curricula, and provide on-the-job training. It will also require forging new relationships for developing talent by, for instance, engaging with entrepreneurs and technology developers, partnering with educational institutions, and collaborating with policy makers.

U.S. utilities companies have already begun doing this. In 2006 they joined forces to establish the Center for Energy Workforce Development. The mission of the center, which has no physical office and is staffed primarily by former employees from member companies, is to figure out what jobs and skills the industry will need most as its older workers retire—and then how best to create a pipeline to meet those needs. "We're used to working together in this industry," Ann Randazzo, the center's executive director, told us. "When there's a storm, everybody gets in their trucks. Even if we compete in certain areas, including for workers, we've all got to work together to build this pipeline, or there just aren't going to be enough people."

The center quickly determined that three of the industry's most critical middle-skills jobs—linemen, field operators, and energy technicians—would be hit hard by the retirement of workers in the near future. Together, those three jobs make up almost 40% of a typical utility's workforce. To make sure they wouldn't go unfilled, CEWD implemented a two-pronged strategy. It created detailed tool kits, curricula, and training materials for all three jobs, which it made available free to utility companies; and it launched a grassroots movement to reach out to next-generation workers and promote careers in the industry.

CEWD believes in connecting with promising talent early—very early. To that end, it has been working with hundreds of elementary, middle, and high schools to create materials and programs that introduce students to the benefits of working in the industry. These include a sense of larger purpose (delivering critical services to customers); stability (no offshoring of jobs, little technological displacement); the use of automation and technology to make jobs less physically taxing and more intellectually engaging; and, last but not least, surprisingly high wages. Describing the program to us, Randazzo said, "You're *growing* a workforce. We had to start from scratch to get students in the lower grades to understand what they need to do and to really be able to grow that all the way through high school to community colleges and universities. And it's not a one-and-done. We have to continually nurture it."

5. Find ways to manage chronic uncertainty

In today's world, managers know that if they don't swiftly identify and respond to shifts, their companies will be left behind. So how can firms best prepare?

The office-furniture manufacturer Steelcase has come up with some intriguing ideas. One is its Strategic Workforce Architecture and Transformation (SWAT) team, which tracks emerging trends and conducts real-time experiments in how to respond to them. The team has launched an internal platform called Loop, for example, where employees can volunteer to work on projects outside their own functions. This benefits both the company and its employees: As new needs arise, the company can quickly locate workers within its ranks who have the motivation and skills to meet them, and workers can gain experience and develop new capabilities in ways that their current jobs simply don't allow.

Employees at Steelcase have embraced Loop, and its success illustrates an idea that came through very clearly in our survey results. As Jill Dark, the director of the SWAT team, put it to us, "If you give people the opportunity to learn something new or to show their craft, they will give you their best work. The magic is in providing the opportunity."

That's a lesson that all managers should heed.

Originally published in May–June 2019. Reprint R1903H

About the Contributors

KENTARO ARAMAKI is the leader of Egon Zehnder's Executive Assessment and Development Practice in Japan.

DOMINIC BARTON is the global managing partner of McKinsey & Company. He is a coauthor of *Talent Wins: The New Playbook for Putting People First* (Harvard Business Review Press, 2018).

RICHARD W. BEATTY is a professor of human resource management at Rutgers University. He is a coauthor of *The Workforce Scorecard* (Harvard Business Review Press, 2005) and *The Differentiated Workforce* (Harvard Business Review Press, 2009).

BRIAN E. BECKER is a professor of human resources in the School of Management at SUNY Buffalo in New York. He is a coauthor of *The Workforce Scorecard* and *The Differentiated Workforce*.

MARCUS BUCKINGHAM is the head of people and performance research at the ADP Research Institute and a coauthor of *Nine Lies About Work: A Freethinking Leader's Guide to the Real World* (Harvard Business Review Press, 2019).

PETER CAPPELLI is the George W. Taylor Professor of Management at the Wharton School and a director of its Center for Human Resources. He is the author of several books, including *Will College Pay Off? A Guide to the Most Important Financial Decision You'll Ever Make.*

DENNIS CAREY is the vice chair of Korn Ferry. He is the coauthor of seven books, including *Talent, Strategy, Risk: How Investors and Boards Are Redefining TSR* (Harvard Business Review Press, 2021) and *Talent Wins: The New Playbook for Putting People First* (Harvard Business Review Press, 2018). He has recruited for boards and CEOs across the U.S.

ALICE DE CHALENDAR is a consultant at BCG and a researcher at the BCG Henderson Institute.

RAM CHARAN advises the CEOs and boards of some of the world's biggest corporations and serves on seven boards himself. He is the author or coauthor of many books, including *Talent, Strategy, Risk* (Harvard Business Review Press, 2021) and *Talent Wins* (Harvard Business Review Press, 2018).

CLAUDIO FERNÁNDEZ-ARÁOZ is an executive fellow for executive education at Harvard Business School and the author of *It's Not the How or the What but the Who* (Harvard Business Review Press, 2014).

ANDY FLEMING is the CEO of The Development Edge and a coauthor of *An Everyone Culture: Becoming a Deliberately Developmental Organization* (Harvard Business Review Press, 2016).

JOSEPH FULLER is a professor of management practice and a cochair of the Project on Managing the Future of Work at Harvard Business School. He is also the faculty cochair of HBS's executive education program on Leading an Agile Workforce Transformation.

ASHLEY GOODALL is senior vice president of leadership and team intelligence at Cisco Systems and a coauthor of *Nine Lies About Work* (Harvard Business Review Press, 2019).

LYNDA GRATTON is a professor of management practice at London Business School and the founder of HSM, the future-of-work research consultancy. Her most recent book, coauthored with Andrew J. Scott, is *The New Long Life: A Framework for Flourishing in a Changing World.*

LINDA A. HILL is the Wallace Brett Donham Professor of Business Administration at Harvard Business School. She is the author of *Becoming a Manager* (Harvard Business Review Press, 2019), and a coauthor of *Being the Boss* (Harvard Business Review Press, 2019), and *Collective Genius* (Harvard Business Review Press, 2014).

MARK A. HUSELID is a professor and director of the Center for Workforce Analytics at Northeastern University. He is a coauthor of *The Workforce Scorecard* and *The Differentiated Workforce*.

ROBERT KEGAN is the William and Miriam Meehan Professor of Adult Learning and Professional Development at the Harvard Graduate School of Education.

LISA LAHEY is a lecturer at the Harvard Graduate School of Education and the cofounder and chief knowledge officer of The Development Edge.

ANTHONY J. MAYO is the Thomas S. Murphy Senior Lecturer of Business Administration in the Organizational Behavior unit of Harvard Business School.

MATTHEW MILLER is a lecturer and the associate dean for learning and teaching at the Harvard Graduate School of Education.

MANJARI RAMAN is a program director and senior researcher for Harvard Business School's Project on U.S. Competitiveness and the Project on Managing the Future of Work.

DOUGLAS A. READY is a senior lecturer at MIT's Sloan School of Management and the founder and president of ICEDR.

LAURA MORGAN ROBERTS is a professor of practice at the University of Virginia's Darden School of Business and coeditor of *Race, Work and Leadership: New Perspectives on the Black Experience* (Harvard Business Review Press, 2019).

ANDREW ROSCOE is the former leader of Egon Zehnder's Executive Assessment and Development Practice.

ANNA TAVIS is a clinical associate professor of human capital management at New York University and the "Perspectives" editor at *People + Strategy*, a journal for HR executives.

ROBERT J. THOMAS is a managing director of Accenture Strategy. He is the author of eight books on leadership and organizational change, including *Crucibles of Leadership, Geeks and Geezers* (with Warren Bennis), and *Driving Results through Social Networks* (with Robert L. Cross).

JUDITH K. WALLENSTEIN is a senior partner and managing director at Boston Consulting Group and a BCG Fellow.

Index

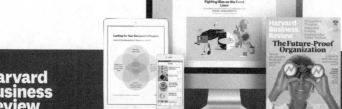